What Others Are Saying About Charlene Ann...

"Charlene has the charm of putting ... trivial of experiences ... making t... a window was opening from a narrow tunnel—and ahead were shiny spots of joy ... making even what could be dull and drab take on an appearance of brightness."

—Barbara Johnson, author of *Splashes of Joy in the Cesspools of Life*

"Charlene's outrageous humor will tickle you with life-giving laughter!"

—Patsy Clairmont, author of *God Uses Cracked Pots* and *Under His Wings*

"What you do helps so many to rise above the heaviness of life, and live and laugh and face another day, so thanks!!!!"

—Loreen, Inner Grove Heights, MN

"I thought that my 'colourful' past was holding me back. . . . What I took from your message was that I am okay as I am. That a Christian woman doesn't have to look or act a certain way."

—Don't Miss Your Life! seminar attendee

"Thank you so very much for reminding me that stressful situations can be laughable while I'm actually having one."

—Don't Miss Your Life! seminar attendee

"Masterfully woven together humor and the truth about God and our need for Him."

—Don't Miss Your Life! seminar attendee

"Having tired of superficial, smile-so-sweetly Christianity, I found Charlene Baumbich to be a breath (rather a strong wind) of fresh air. I love learning from someone who has outrageously trusted Christ in the gut-level issues of life."

—Wild Child of God seminar attendee

"What a blessing to be encouraged to be genuine with other women and to again be told how much God loves us—while being challenged to be on fire for God."

—Wild Child of God seminar attendee

Charlene Ann Baumbich

Don't miss Your Life!

An Uncommon Guide to Living with Freedom, Laughter, and Grace

HOWARD BOOKS
A DIVISION OF SIMON & SCHUSTER

Our purpose at Howard Books is to:
·*Increase faith* in the hearts of growing Christians
·*Inspire holiness* in the lives of believers
·*Instill hope* in the hearts of struggling people everywhere
Because He's coming again!

Published by Howard Books, a division of Simon & Schuster, Inc.
1230 Avenue of the Americas, New York, NY 10020
www.howardpublishing.com

Published in association with Danielle Egan-Miller of Browne & Miller Literary Associates.

[First Howard trade paperback edition June 2009]

Library of Congress Cataloging-in-Publication Data

Baumbich, Charlene Ann, 1945–
  Don't miss your life! : an uncommon guide to living with freedom, laughter, and grace / Charlene Ann Baumbick. — 1st Howard Books trade pbk. ed.
    p. cm.
Includes bibliographical references.
1. Christian life. I. Title.
BV4501.3.B395 2009
204'.4—dc22

                                                                                        2008048372

ISBN-13: 978-1-4165-6299-3
ISBN-10:   1-4165-6299-0
10 9 8 7 6 5 4 3 2 1

Manufactured in the United States of America

For information regarding special discounts for bulk purchases, please contact: Simon & Schuster Special Sales at 1-866-506-1949 or business@simonandschuster.com.

The Simon & Schuster Speakers Bureau can bring authors to your live event. For more information or to book an event contact the Simon & Schuster Speakers Bureau at 866-248-3049 or visit our website at www.simonspeakers.com.

Book design by Jessica Shatan Heslin/Studio Shatan, Inc.

Dedicated to:

The brave writers who dared to reveal their Real Selves on the page, and in doing so, influenced and encouraged me to do the same. At the time of this writing, these dear folks and works come especially to mind.

MADELEINE L'ENGLE, whose book *Walking on Water: Reflections on Faith and Art* helped me to get over myself.

FREDERICK BUECHNER, whose compilation *Listening to Your Life: Daily Meditations with Frederick Buechner* introduced me to his remarkable self.

MIKE YACONELLI, whose fearless honesty inspired me as I repeatedly said, "Yeah, baby!" while reading *Messy Spirituality*.

RAY BRADBURY, whose freeing work *Zen in the Art of Writing: Essays on Creativity* utterly rocks.

ANNE LAMOTT, whose nonfiction tickles my *Ha-ha-ha!* zone, awakens my wonder, and kicks me where I need kicking. *Traveling Mercies: Some Thoughts on Faith* is way more important than "some thoughts." (Expect laughter, insight, grace, true life, and rough language in this book, because you'll get them.)

Contents

Jacob was a reed,

and the breath of God

blew through Jacob,

made music of him.

—*Jacob the Baker* by Noah benShea

Disclaimer

This book cannot take the place of a psychiatrist, a therapist, or a zoologist. (Yes, sometimes life seems that wild—and not in a good way.) If you are consumed by a major issue, one that requires serious professional help, consider yourself strong enough to take a stand and seek it. Although I've survived being a den mother (I'm convinced that den-mothering skills prepare you to rule the world) whose scouts once tried to kill me in my own basement by all passing gas at the same time, which surely qualifies me for *something*, this courageous "training" does not substitute for degreed people who can counsel you back to strong mental health. So go to them.

But percolate the ideas in this book as companions to your counseling. At the very least, hold some of your own stories up against mine. No doubt you'll find yourself saying, "Good grief! If *that's* 'normal,' I'm not as far off base as I think!"

Introduction

Du001ring a casual, roundtable dinner gathering with an eclectic group of people (and just so you know, I, myself, am a *bundle* of eclectic rolled into one fluffy midlifer's body), the topic of those who've gone before us and how their deaths affected our lives began taking root. The nature of the stories ran the emotional gamut. They ranged from a couple who'd lost their son (*Lord, protect my children!*), to barely known relatives, to friends and foes who'd influenced our lives for the better and the dubious. They also included a few downright wacky funeral stories. We were reminded that laughter in the midst of all things funereal is a healing grace. And since your curiosity is undoubtedly piqued, I promise to share one of those stories later.

Aside from myself, most people at the table knew one another, so I mostly listened to the first few rounds of exchanges. But after a while, I felt the gentle persuasive winds of that "great cloud of witnesses" who have gone before me starting to circle close by, pressing in, tapping me on the shoulder with *their* stories. I opened myself to my table companions by sharing how my mom had died at only fifty-six years of age, *my* exact age at the time of the discussion. "I'm so glad she modeled to me what it looks like to really *live*," I said with thankfulness and conviction. "I can't imagine having endured living in the aftermath of her stroke and quick death if I'd spent the rest of *my* life knowing Mom had been waiting to start *hers*."

The mother across the table from me (the mother who'd lost her son) leaned in and with an immediate and urgent intensity in her voice asked, "What do you mean by that?" Like a coonhound that picks up the scent of its desire, she went on high alert, ready to track, chase, and corner this "really live" trail. She was prepared to keep me treed until she got what she wanted, which was details delivered through stories. Stories of life to the full from which she could extract her own applications.

She had a need.

Let me be perfectly clear here: *I* cannot fill either her or anyone else's need. But through the grace and power of story as testimony, God can, and often does, anoint the messages within them. What else could explain such personal interpretation, extrapolation, and applications *from* them? Therefore, I believe stories from my mother's life—from *each* of our lives—possess holy and hope-filled example, perspective, possibilities, and joy.

The woman explained that since shortly after the accidental death of their young adult son some years previously, she and her husband, who nodded his head throughout her explanation, found themselves processing their responses to *life* in very different manners. Another friend of mine, who'd also lost a son, once explained that although you never get over the pain, you do learn to live with it. So, too, this grieving mother was able to draw a clear distinction between the cause and effect of grief following a death, and the intentional pursuit of life.

For better or for worse, for the taking or the leaving, death's fierce blindsiding also births unique truths regarding the fragility and palpable presence of life.

She went on to explain that not long after they buried their son, her husband decided to fulfill a longtime dream: buy a motorcycle, learn how to use it, and fearlessly—dared she say irresponsibly? (yes, she did)—ride like the wind. She, however, now spent a great portion of her waking hours fearing for his safety and the well-being of their daughter. One loss was already more than she could bear; they all needed to be careful, cautious, attentive—together. Can you feel her own fear threatening to shrink-wrap them? Perhaps you're familiar with the sensation. But the mere mention of my mother's ability to live life to the full drew her toward something more: a new way.

The loss of a child is an extreme example—of just about anything. But how do the rest of us respond to life's far lesser invasions, surprises, disappointments, and, yes, even victories? Are we awake to life's nuances such as the daring trill of a roadside, weed-riding red-winged blackbird; the size of your right pinkie finger's moon (to those of you wearing acrylics, sorry); the shadow of doubt that crosses your lover's face; the shaft of light on your desk; the small puff of your nursing baby's breath upon your breast; the joy-filled ripple effect of a song heard on the radio, later hummed that night, and a grown woman's sheer joy remembering that mother's hum, long after her beloved mother has departed this earth?

So it was—and is—for me as I savor the memory of my mother's vibrating, vibrant sound. More than three decades after her death, I still hear my mother humming. Bless you, Mom, for leaving me with the sound of a hallowed, sparkling, rich, and full life.

My prayer for you (seriously, I am praying for you as I type) is that you use the pages of this book to discover your own rich and sustaining memories, then learn how to use them as a springboard to live life to its fullest. Above all, don't *miss* your life! With a little thought and practice, you, too, can wholly partake of each sacred moment.

I *remember when?

What We Already Know

> **MEMORY PORTFOLIO (MP):** Your invisible, utterly personal, wholly accessible, always-ready-for-new-entries, combination diary and scrapbook of sensory-loaded captured moments. Properly honored, added to, mined, evaluated, sifted, and, sometimes even edited, gentle examination of said captured moments can become the key—the very path—to your success in not *missing* your life.

When I was a child, I loved playing spaceship and building worm forts with the Cook brothers. They lived just up the path through the weeds—the path we'd created by endlessly running through them. (Cook brothers, if you're out there, please contact me! My maiden name was Brown.) We once left this earth (for *real*) on an abandoned hot-water heater rigged with a control panel made of half-melted camera flash cubes and pieces of wood that we wired and taped to its side. Of course this was back in the pre-Wii days, when our only option was to engage in real-life hands-on play, like sifting through the remnants of the garbage our folks burned in a rusty barrel out back. Where else could we discover a once-common flash cube transformed by fire into a crystal launch button?

During our space explorations, I was always Flash Gordon.[1] I mean to tell you, I *was* Flash Gordon, neither a pretend Flash nor one of those froufrou tight-clothed girls in the old black-and-white television show of my youth. Nope, I was Flash, who was also tight-clothed, but not in "that" way. As for the worm forts, they were exquisite—although I do not recommend putting a swimming pool in your complex. Don't ask me how I know.

Over time, I became a Gypsy (inspired by the exotic Sophia Loren), Annie Oakley[2] (sharpshooter), Calamity Jane[3] (rough-and-tumble), Crazy Googenheim (I *loved* making my mother laugh while pretending to be that wonderful character brought to life by Frank Fontaine on *The Jackie Gleason Show*), and Doris Day, that quirky fanny-swinging dame of a movie star with whom men always fell in love. A comparable cast for today's youth—or, on a bad day at the office or with the kids—perhaps might be made up of an actual astronaut (we didn't yet have them back in the fifties), Cameron Diaz, Drew Barrymore, or, say, Jim Carrey.

Although I wasn't doing typical childhood writerly things like reading stacks of books or writing, not even in a diary, I always had a story running in my head. I was too busy "living" in another world or paying attention to the fine, wondrous, confounding, and startling details of my own life to sit down and write about it. At the time, little did I know that my natural childhood inclination to live in "otherly" skin was setting the stage for my all-growed-up, as my grandma used to say, "accidental" fiction-writing career. Never did I suspect that my youthful God-given instinct to pay close attention to the physical and emotional nuances of my own life, as well as the lives of those around me, was preparing me for one of the most fulfilling and rewarding joys of my *entire* life: writing this book. However, during an astute memory portfolio (MP) review, my writerly path and this burning message became as clear as a bell. When we give our MPs a chance to work for us, what obvious and meaningful threads we discover woven throughout them! Not only that, but what might the patterns of our frayed threads teach us—spare us from in the future—if we learned to recognize and heed their warning stitches?

Turns out I am best fed, educated, and ministered to by the magical, mystical power unleashed through stories, and hugely blessed by passing them along. I'm also often a complete doofus, a "qualification" God uses to make sure I don't run out of fun and wholly relatable, so I'm told time and again, material. *Thank you, God—I think.* That is why I'm offering *you* this easygoing pluck-and-play opportunity to pluck what you want from this book of stories and play their implications and possibilities into your life as needed. Be advised that along with a full exploration of your MP, a strong *Play!* thread will weave its way throughout these pages. Doesn't this approach add up to more fun than a scary "self-help" theme?

Then the Lord God formed man of dust from the ground, and breathed into his nostrils the breath of life; and man became a living being.

GENESIS 2:7 NASB

In the most relaxing, amusing, yet thought-provoking ways possible, I want to remind you, (and me, too) of an incredible asset you've been given. I'm talking a mega-asset that is so easy to forget. Ready? Here it is: your one and only, true-self—not someone else's version/vision—God-breathed life. I don't know how we can forget such an easy-to-remember asset, but we do. So, if you feel like you've lost your way, or like you might need an emotional laxative for your fun-impaired, spiritually consti-pated, fear-laden self, this message is just the painless (well, mostly) ticket to help you get your life back to YOUR LIFE!

'Tis my quest to help you learn the lively and releasing arts of listening to, mining, and then sharing your *own* stories. Yes, even *that* story that you hoped you'd never have to think about again, since maybe, just maybe, you can at long last learn to laugh about it, or at least unknot the emotional ties that feed its life-nabbing viral-ness.

❋ ❋ ❋

If you explore your happiest childhood memories of times at play with your friends, I believe you will discover that they reveal the same keys that can infuse you with satisfaction today. This is one of the best features of an MP, demonstrated by the fact that when I say something like "Explore your happi-est childhood memories," you *can*. Your MP is already up and running and contains everything you need. Although it might require an occasional reboot or memory tickler—and I'm going to deliver tons of them—no new software is required. Just dive in! In fact, do it right *now*! Shine a light around in the alcoves of your childhood when you were playing with your favorite play-mates.

You are searching, remembering, rediscovering, reawakening . . .

What did you find? Did you spend the majority of your youthful playtime with your *imaginary* friend? Well, that counts. If you thought, perhaps *still* think, that imaginary friends are completely weird and unheard of in your land of play, well, that counts, too. After all, it is your brain, your life.

But the universal truth is this: whether our true friends were born of our imaginations or our childhoods or we cultivated them as adults, they can serve as mirrors and stabilizers, partners and butt-kickers, examples and lessons in our lives. Those voices from the past, trusted friends in the present, and conversations regarding our futures can often guide us back to our personal North Star course, which we might have long ago lost in the shuffle. Please try to consider *me* one of your new friends, for that is the spirit I bring to this book.

Are you unhappy in your current vocation? Perhaps something as easy as perusing your MP and pondering your natural gifts, attributes, and leanings can point you toward a new, more satisfying career, or at least flush out a fresh, rejuvenating, and fulfilling avocation or hobby. Later, I'm going to help you examine the "way" you used to play before someone encouraged you to start "applying" yourself, which often implied you should knuckle down and leave your natural-bent "fun and frivolous"—HA!—inclinations behind. Your MP is a great place to search for the gifts you've lost or set aside, to lift them to the light and reignite them.

What if you don't even know if you *have* any gifts? Suggestion: listen, mouth zipped, to the way your friends, both old and new, can lay out your strengths. If you don't believe me, ask them. It's time you shore up and reclaim your uniqueness, if, somewhere along the line, you handed it over to the blandness of *other* people's expectations for you. It's time to reignite the God-given hope you already harbor within.

But if we hope for what we do not see, with

perseverance we wait eagerly for it.

ROMANS 8:25 NASB

Hope is perhaps the first key that can enable you to wake up, then open up, to your life. Without hope, we are left with only despair. As I heard—and forever remembered—Marilla Cuthbert say to Anne Shirley in the 1985 made-for-TV adaption of *Anne of Green Gables,* "To despair is to turn your back on God." Now, who's gutsy enough to do that?! Not I!

❉❋❉

Maybe you derailed (hey, you picked up this book, so *something* must have happened!) when you began assuming your life is worse than its actuality. Our assumptions can get us into whole heaps of trouble, not to mention waste big blocks of our valuable time here on this earth. How often have you stood in the line you assumed to be the correct line, only to learn upon finally arriving at the clerk that you've wasted your time in the *wrong* line? How many times have you assumed something about your spouse, say, that she'd like a can opener for her birthday or that he'd welcome a subscription to *Communicating 101* as a good change of pace, only to learn you were wrong—by a gazillion miles? And not only that, you're now in deep doo-doo, bucko or buckette. How often do you set a course for your career, project, or parenting skills based on assumptions that one of those well-known and respected gurus, including the ones on television, is actually correct about your individual situation? And surely they wouldn't let people have their own *TV* shows if they didn't know what they were talking about! *Would* they? Never mind that he or she knows none of the details about *your* personal life. So you follow their advice to the letter, only to receive a gut punch to your psyche when your leap of assumption dumps you and your loved ones down the proverbial drain. Again.

But even if my examples of errant assumptions *did* feel like personal excerpts out of your past year (*doink!*), be of good cheer since you, you smart *smart* person, are reading this book. I'm going to deliver handles and stories that can help you learn the vital art of questioning your assumptions. [MOMENT OF TRUTH: You're on your own with those story lines.] Together, we will tame a few shrewish thoughts and ignite more noble ones. And if that's not already a deal for the price, I'm even going to help you question your questions! For instance, in your valiant attempts to find out why your life's trolley has slipped off its happy track, perhaps you're asking yourself, *Why can't I be more like [fill in the blank]?*

BZZZZZZZZZZ! Wrong question! God and I are here to meet you exactly where, how, and *who* you are, which reminds me of a story logged in my MP that well illustrates my point. See how this is going to work?

❋ ❋ ❋

I love to attend stock-car races held on half-mile dirt tracks. My favorite part? The glorious crescendo of rumbling thunder that comes rippin' 'round turn four when the drivers see the track lights turn green. Previous to that moment, perhaps they've had to circle the track once or twice, arranging and rearranging themselves until they jostle to the track official's liking, but then . . . GO! As opposed to the "cleanliness" of NASCAR races, I adore the remarkable demonstration of *energy* when, depending on track conditions, either dust or mud kicks out from behind the tires as the metal-to-metal mass—or perhaps only two cars that have broken away from the pack—makes its way past the roar of the crazed crowd. Heart pounding, I sit in awe of each driver who dives into the turns (Man, I wish I was *him*!), exploding the back end of his or her car into a wider-skidding arc than that of the curb-hugging front end. Centrifugal poetry set to motion by wild childs! Oh, baby! Although I feel bad for those who, on their own accord, spin out, I also secretly revel in their courage, since it means they held nothing back. Full bore. Head-on. Havin' at it! No put-puttin' for *them*! Isn't that the way you want to go through life?

Years ago, the grand-finale race at a track not too far from us was a "Run What You Brung" event. (No doubt insurance eventually shut it down.) In other words, if you're revved up from watching the night's action (Let me at it!) and want to give it a whirl yourself, go ahead and line up your street car—the one you drove to the races—for the "Run What You Brung." To be fair, you probably had to prepare for this before the actual event since your car needed to be in the pits, and there were no doubt indemnity waivers. But nonetheless, you "raced" your street-drivin' vehicle. [MOMENT OF TRUTH: Most nights for this event, the word *race* was a gross exaggeration since gutsy racing appears easier than it is, but buddy, by golly they were *in* it!]

So, too, all *you* need to begin *this* journey into not missing your life is to run what you brung. You need no further preparation than to show up, which you've already done. If you're happy and you know it, drive yer happy self right on up to the starting line. If you're lost and you show it, you, too, are on the right track since you're seeking a better way. So you see, you don't need to be more like somebody else; you just need to be whoever—and however—you are at this very moment.

Is anyone among you suffering? Let him pray. Is anyone cheerful? Let him sing praises. James 5:13 (ESV). Notice that doesn't say snap out of it, shut up, or go away. Kinda sounds like God's "run what ya brung!" permission slip to me. *Amen!*

❋ ❋ ❋

When I first started coming to grips with the fact that I'd "accidentally" (more on this later) become a *professional* speaker, a *professional* writer (Stand back! Professional words at work here!), I couldn't for the life of me believe it. [MOMENT OF TRUTH: To this day, only God can truly explain how I got so "lucky"!] For years, every stumbling step of the writerly/speakerly way, I kept thinking, *When are they going to discover I don't know what I'm doing? When will someone finally check my report cards and learn I received average grades in all things English? How is it that editors at publishing houses, newspapers, and magazines have chosen to publish my articles and books instead of many others written by people who've spent their lives doing all the right things to become published writers, like write-write-writing stories from the time they were little, keeping a diary or journaling every day, attending journalism school . . . none of which is in my history? How is it that kind folks pay me to come speak at their events when I have no degrees in anything?* Other than a couple miscellaneous writing classes, an unending passion to share what I've learned, and more guts than brains, I have no certifiable qualifications to do what I do. Oh, and that "mostly Irish" thing, which not only honors Story but believes in Story's innate power to transform.

But when I examined my childhood adventures with my

friends, the writing (hahahaha) was on the wall. Or rather it was lurking in the gifts God gave to me—none of which I earned or deserved—along with an unignorable lure to *play* with them. (Ah, we're back to the pluck-and-play mantra of this book. Nice!) Of course when I was a child, I had no inkling about "gifts," nor did anyone pressure me to use them. *Thank you, Mom, Dad!* I had no drive to find a career path; my mom was so happy in her home-maker role that all I wanted was to one day get married and have kids, too, which is what I did. My parents weren't channeling all their energies into pushing me down the "fast track" so I could attend the "right" college. *Thank you and bless you, Mom and Dad.* (Don't get me *started* on the topic of parental pressuring!) Aside from school, household chores, horses to feed, and stalls to shovel, I had no demands. I simply had time to play at what-ever floated my boat, whispered to my creative brain, delighted my unstressed heart. I had leisure time (which overbooked kids do not have—okay, I started anyway, but I promise that I'm done now—I hope!) to explore my natural bents using the crude "tools" of childhood that would one day help hone my happiness and ability to fully live.

✻✿✻

I n that last paragraph, you likely noticed that I tried not to get *started* on something that launches me up on a soapbox—and not in a good way. (If you didn't notice, *wake up*, people! Thank-fully, the next chapter is about wakefulness, but at least flut-ter your eyes to let me know you're still with me—and yourself.) Sadly, I failed at my attempt to stifle myself since only three sen-tences later, I *started*! Is that kind of lack-of-self-disciplined failure familiar to you? At least this time, even though I sorrily *started*, I was able to quickly *stop* myself. [MOMENT OF TRUTH:

I'm getting better at catching myself. Just not always.] The encouraging part for all of us is this: as opposed to the negativity of my soapbox, I also possess, and later will share, many positive, productive antidotes and inspirations on the topic of overbooked *anyone*, especially *ourselves*.

Summing it all up, friends [emphasis mine], *I'd say you'll do best by filling your minds and meditating on things true, noble, reputable, authentic, compelling, gracious—the best, not the worst; the beautiful, not the ugly; things to praise, not things to curse. Put into practice what you learned from me, what you heard and saw and realized. Do that, and God, who makes everything work together, will work you into his most excellent harmonies.*

PHILIPPIANS 4:8,9 MSG

All of us possess our good sides, as well as our shadowy soapbox-y [or fill-in-the-blank] sides. Again, here's where our MPs usher forth yet another great incentive to explore them: I don't want to one day open mine and discover that every page is filled with me ranting. I feel assured you don't want that type of over-riding vibe in your MP either. But here's one of the truly great things about life: right this moment, God is with us. Because God is with us and holds us close, we therefore each possess the power—God's power—to make our new MP entries more posi-tive. *Wonderful!* I'd much rather remember, and be remembered for, my helpful attributes than my negative, harmful, or sarcastic ones, wouldn't you?

So, even though we mess up, we're here to run what we brung with the hope that we can, and will, get better, especially if and when we let our MPs tutor us while God holds our hands and hearts.

We find what we look for, so let's look for what's right—including in ourselves. How can we move forward in our lives if we're using all of our energy pounding ourselves and others downward?

❊❊❊

Throughout these pages, I'm going to share many stories from my journey. They will run the gamut between hysterical (both ha-ha! and oh, *no!*), pristine, tormenting, profound, *Duh!*, and beautiful. I have no doubt that within them, you will connect with the good, bad, and dubious shades of *yourself*. As you read, pluck, and play along, you'll be able to apply some order, meaning, and a tad of funk-tionality to *your* memory portfolio and discover that your days are, or soon can be, indeed better than you think.

God called his creation and everything in it—which includes us—good. Even when we behave badly and fall short and say stupid stuff, we are loved by God. Put it in your memory port-folio and bring it along. It will be the most important thing you need to remember. But do yourself a favor: stop every few pages and *pray* for your own stories, memories, and joys to rise to the surface. Be willing to put the book down when they do, close your eyes, and allow yourself to sink into them. When you read about *me* second-thinking things or questioning an assumption, you do the same. Sometimes those double-clutch discoveries are both startling and illuminating. Perhaps they'll even be life transforming.

In fact, let's practice. Stop and pray right now. Pray that God illuminates everything—all the lessons, options, goodness, and choices—you need to extract, then trust his grace to help you pray and play it into your life.

(You're supposed to be praying!)

Amen.

2 ✳ wake up!

A Call to Attentiveness

Do your days just seem to pass by in a blur, one melding into the next? Like many of us in the midst of our hurry-hurry existence, we thirst to be living life to the full, but first we need to be stunned into realizing how asleep we've been—especially in the midst of our distracting busyness.

For instance, have you ever been driving down the road and . . . OH! I don't remember driving the last five blocks! How did I get here?

When speaking at conferences, I often ask this question; then I ask how many people have experienced this odd phenomenon. I'd say at least 75 percent of the folks raise a hand. And proudly, too. Which is kinda scary (okay, really scary) since look how many of us don't have a clue what we're doing while we're behind the wheel! I'd guess the other 25 percent are either too embarrassed to admit to such insanity or, more likely, are still "driving those five blocks" when I ask the question. The loud burst of laughter shocks them into *their* "how did I get *here*?" moment, but by then, it's already too late to be counted among the normal (?) majority in the room. Or flee, in case they've also just awakened to the fact they're at the wrong lecture.

Life too often passes us by while we're "zoned." Five blocks. Five weeks. I can't believe I'm flipping the calendar page again! Where did the past year go? Oh, my golly: I just got my invitation to join AARP! What is happening to my life?

If you've just asked yourself that last question (and maybe even answered it), good for you. It's the beginning of getting your life back. It's time to begin looking through your own mental lost-and-found piles and saying "Oh! *Here* my life is!" Far better to ask the "What's happening to my life?" question now than to have it assault you on your deathbed. *This can't be the end! I was just waiting for the [fill in the blank] to finally come along, fall into place, or finish up so I could start living!* The reality is, most likely we won't know when that closing curtain will snuff us out, so wake up!

I have come that they might have life,

and have it to the full.

John 10:10 NIV

Determine that *you* will become the one your friends and family say really *lived*.

✻❄✻

Several years ago my husband, George, and I attended a family gathering in Cleveland. Aside from either a few driving or airport pass-throughs, I'd never been to the Forest City. Before I booked our reservations, I decided to scan the Internet to see what fun things I could find. I thought a new discovery might influence the length of our stay, which, in George's mind, was overnight. Hear him sigh when I mention the great and *exciting* potential we have to turn our simple trip into an *extravaganza*! After nearly forty years of marriage—read sighing—I'm surprised his body hasn't completely deflated by now. [MOMENT OF TRUTH: After enduring forty years of marriage to *me*, obviously the man is a saint.] A Google search brought up the Rock and Roll Hall of Fame and Museum. (Hear George sigh.) Plans were made, and off we went.

I loved the Rock and Roll Hall of Fame and Museum (R&R HoF), every square inch of it. We stayed 7.5 hours (yes, the man is a saint) and we left then only because it was closing. Still, I missed several things. Did you know you can look up just about any song that's ever been recorded and play it? Since I write for a living as well as for my own sanity, I spent careful time reading framed, original hand-scrawled songs, complete with lined-out edits; letters; inside-business tidbits . . . It was an amazing opportunity to study some of the familiar and genuine—not to mention genuinely bedazzling—stage costumes of famous stars. Some of the bigger-than-life personalities were, in fact, much smaller in stature than I realized, and vice versa. Diverse multimedia exhibits were built around personalities, each of whom, in small or large part, framed my appreciation for music, which is a potent force in my life. So powerful is my need for music that I sometimes think if I opened a vein, blood wouldn't spurt out but notes would pour forth, creating new melodies as they danced their way into the cosmos.

"But now bring me a minstrel." And it came about, when the minstrel played, that the hand of the Lord came upon him.

2 KINGS 3:15 NASB

While I was drinking of the historical wealth harbored in the R&R HoF, a theme began to emerge in my consciousness. Throughout rock and roll's history, hundreds of performers and songwriters sadly and tragically flared out before their time because of negative excesses such as drugs. They inadvertently surrounded themselves with money-grabbing people who didn't look out for them, but who instead *fed* their excesses. Even so, the majority of the rockers seemed intent on saying one thing to their generation: *wake up!* Here in the R&R HoF, the assemblage of the remnants of these artists' *stories* are held sacred as pilot lights to help us ignite *our* memories, *our* stories. I once heard Lynn Redgrave say, "A good story has the power to heal the soul." Yes, a good story is a wonder-filled, motivating (motivating = key word, in case you missed it), and healing balm. Even the saddest stories about some of these performers hold the power to help us wake up, take stock of *our* positive and negative influences, and live better lives. In the end, bad examples are nonetheless examples.

An advertisement for Southwest Airlines, "Official Airline of the Essence Music Festival"—at least it was this the year I read about it in a magazine—said, "Scientists don't have instruments to measure the human soul. But musicians do." *Amen!* It's amazing how many latent recesses of our personal lives can be illuminated by inspiring, challenging, sweet, invading, screaming, or seductive melodies and lyrics. Want to wake up a few memories? Head to the R&R HoF, Graceland, or the Country Western Hall of Fame and Museum. Tune in to an oldies radio station or your own stash of vintage music, which in my case even includes vinyls. If you listen—really listen—I bet at least one out of every ten songs will spring forth in your MP to remind you of a time, day, or moment gone by. If the song washes up a good era or memory, play it again and again until the more fuzzy-edged images come back into focus. If it's not a good memory or you just hate the song, there's always the on/off button, fast-forward (I can think of a few times in my life where that kind of time-traveling mechanism would have saved me a wad of embarrassment), skip disk, or fine tuning, which, as we age—and if we're staying awake to the nuances—becomes more, shall we say, finely tuned.

Therefore my harp is turned to mourning,

And my flute to the sound of those who weep.

Job 30:31 NASB

Yes, let's say that.

If the music helps you cry, perhaps *that's* what you need to do before you can move on.

❖❖❖

If we're awake and not traveling the planet on autopilot, even the new stories we collect as they're happening remind us of our old stories, which then ultimately function as tabbed *sections* in our MPs. My entire first book, *Don't Miss Your Kids! (they'll be gone before you know it)*,[1] was extracted from memories filed in my "child-rearing" section. (Notice a theme to my messages?) My youngest son was a senior in high school when I started penning that book. I recall writing about how quickly the years had flown by, even though some days seemed to last a thousand years. Today that "child" is heading toward forty and is a two-time daddy himself. Ah, the ongoing finger snaps of life! Feel their castanetting rhythm?

After Brian went off to college, I remember the first time he came home for a visit. I was standing at the kitchen window staring at the grammar school across the parkway, the one my sons attended. I heard the stairs creaking and turned to see my rumply-haired, sleepy-eyed "baby" pull out a kitchen chair and plop himself down on it. I stood looking at him, wondering what-all likes and dislikes, habits and opinions had changed about him, what all I didn't know. (As if I knew everything before! HA! My sons *still* love to torment me by divulging things—hideous, *shocking* things—I didn't know back then, many I could happily live without ever having had to know.) Maybe he was a coffee drinker now. I'd heard college is where many learn to drink the dark brew, which I detest but which his dad enjoys. And so I asked.

"What would you like? Are you a coffee drinker now?"

"You know what I'd like, Mom? I'd like a cup of tea with honey."

Oh! My breath caught in my throat and my eyes immediately

began to well with tears. For a moment, I couldn't even speak, so forceful was the arrival of bygone stories . . . moments . . . memories all rolled into one powerful *Oh!* Brian studied my face, then asked me if I'd misunderstood what he'd said, since why else would I be tearing up?

"Oh, *Brian! Tea*, with *honey*!"

"Is this a menopause thing?" he asked. My boys had already heard plenty about me and menopause, hormones, and irrational behaviors.

"No. *No!* It's about . . ." (Sniff. Snort. Collect myself. Search for words to fold the universe into a sentence.) "My mom used to drink tea with honey, and she made *me* tea with honey when I wasn't feeling well. And when you and Bret were little and sick, I made *you* tea and honey. And now you, my man-child, ask me for tea with honey, and it's . . . *everything*." The sudden and overwhelming joy in my heart erupts into an unstoppable river of happy tears, then quickly escalates into a full-blown transcendent episode.

How can I explain to my child that in this moment, I know that I know that I *know* that the sovereign hand of God was on my mother and is on me, and him, and this earth? That the generations of tea-with-honey drinkers in my family symbolize all that is holy and bear witness to such knowledge? I cannot. I can only know it and respond by allowing (as if I could stop it!) my river of tear-laden evidence to pour forth.

And I can grab hold of *that* moment of wakefulness, which thankfully I did, and tuck it in my memory portfolio. When those wondrous insights—those wordless moments of knowing that *you* know—arrive in your life, you, too, can arrive *in* the moment. We can preserve such moments and keep them alive by recalling them often enough so as not to allow them to fade away.

Even though we can perhaps never *feel* that exact moment in the same way again, we can allow the awakened memory of it to guide and sustain us through a terrible time, a dark time, when it's easy to allow ourselves to forget what we know. When we question God's presence in a situation, a person, ourselves.

When we question God's presence.

Who can guess the importance of a seemingly insignificant moment until years later, when it becomes the singular incident that infuses us with clarity, perspective, and the assurance that life is, indeed, better than we think?

But we cannot collect what we are asleep to.

❋ ❋ ❋

Sometimes waking up to life can happen only after a long bout of unwakefulness—literally. Such was the case for me in December of 1995, Friday the thirteenth, which turned out to be a very unlucky and blessed day. It's an MP incident I will never forget—*Please, Lord.* Step with me now *into* that time.

After years of dealing with "issues" surrounding my reproductive system (I shall spare you the glorious, full-color details), I have a decision to make: start getting biopsies twice a year or surgically remove the crabby part, which, in this case, is the uterus. My gynecologist is the conservative type. He doesn't recommend the drastic latter procedure unless said crabbiness of said part threatens my life or the quality of it, which, by this time, it seriously does. "There are always risks with surgery," he says, "and should, God forbid, something happen to you, your family needs to know that your choice to have surgery was the only sensible one." Thus I weigh the options, think about all the times my "normal" life is brought to a halt by my "issues," think about living every day with the threat of cancer and waiting for biopsy results every six months, and then I take the matter to

God in prayer, the same way I always talk to God, which is in my real voice in a real way with my own words.

"God, I'm tired of this crabby old uterus. It's served me well, thank you. Amen." And just like that, the decision is made. Bye-bye uterus and ovaries, contributors to the problem. A couple weeks later, I enter surgery in the late afternoon with readiness and a happy farewell song in my heart. To my uterus, not life.

And then I wake up.

A nurse is standing over me taking my blood pressure. "Well, you sure caused a lot of excitement around here!"

"What do you mean?" I ask through a groggy haze.

"You don't remember?"

"Don't remember what?"

"I'm sure somebody's told you"—she stops talking a moment to listen through the stethoscope, then jots something down—"but the aftereffects of anesthesia have probably caused you to forget. In fact, I *know* you spoke with your husband earlier."

I look around the dark room. "Where *is* my husband?" I ask.

"He went home for the night."

"Night? What time is it?" I can't quite bring the clock on the wall into focus.

"Going on eleven forty-five."

"P.M.?"

She nods, puts her hand on my arm while giving me the short version of my own story. Surgery went well. I was rolled to the recovery room. After the appropriate amount of time, they had trouble arousing me and I said I couldn't feel my legs when they asked me about them. At some point I said I felt sick, then I fell silent again. *Tick-tock.* The nurse checked my monitor, which showed that my heart rate was dropping—and it got all the way down to zero, which astute medical staff deemed too low. CPR was administered. I sprang back to life.

Still somewhat groggy, I struggle to make sense of what she's told me. *I had CPR?* As if checking to see if I truly did survive, I cast my eyes to my legs (check!), notice monitors attached to me here and there (check!). I watch her take my pulse, which seems, thankfully, to be present. It all feels so surreal.

Without the story and its compelling implications, I'm just another woman lying in a bed, and now, because of the incredible story, I am a woman who lives with the knowledge of her own brush with death.

Just then, George, with hesitant steps, walks into the room. He looks scared. He's carrying the foot-tall, hand-knit Postman Pat[2] doll I won at a town raffle (in Colne, Lancashire) during a trip to England three months previously. The doll is precious to me and he knows it will make me happy. What else is there for a husband to bring a wife of twenty-six years after he's almost lost her? After he had to experience such shocking news—long after they'd already told him I'd come through the *surgery* just fine? After he finally dared to go home but then found he couldn't get over his uneasy feeling, and so he needed to come back to the hospital, to sneak in after regulation hospital hours, to see for himself that my heart is still beating . . . for him, for me, for us? What can he bring that will make me smile?

Nothing more perfect than Postman Pat, a souvenir, a *testimony*, to a fulfillment of one of my life's dreams: a trip to England.

The nurse does not give him a lecture about visiting hours being over. On her way out the door, she tells George that I have just learned about "the incident"—since I didn't remember hearing it from him before.

I am so glad to see my husband. I am so glad to see anyone.

I am so glad.

And believe you me, I AM AWAKE TO MY LIFE, which, for the briefest of moments, slipped away.

❖✿❖

Later, after I get over the anesthesia, claim some real sleep, and arrive home (less than twenty-four hours after my heart stopped—the wonders of insurance!), I am also miffed. I cannot believe I missed the most dramatic thing that's ever happened to me! [MOMENT OF TRUTH: I adore drama.] After all, I'd already been preaching my *Don't Miss Your Life!* message for four years, and what a story *this* would make! Such a story, in fact, that after a brief period of recuperation I simply *have* to return to the hospital to meet the nurse whose hands served as the very hands of God and pumped life back into me. I need to see the exact spot where all of this took place. I need *details,* and the scene of the life-giving miracle would help me "see" them.

I need to take in—*take in*—the reality of the fragility of my own life.

❖✿❖

You know, stuff happens to us. Serious stuff. We almost die, or someone we love almost dies—or does. We lose a job. Our best friend moves away. We suffer a spiritual crisis or a personal setback that leaves us reeling. And yet we are so busy, what we have to do is so "important," our schedules so jam-packed, that we just keep moving on.

Or are we perhaps just too afraid to stop and absorb the Terrible Thing for fear we might not be able to deal with it if we thought about it too much?

Did I just hear you say *Ouch!*?

Truthfully, I've thought about every detail of this event many times. For a long while afterward, I couldn't watch a hospital program on TV without picturing myself being the one receiving the pumps for life. I couldn't forget snippets of the conversation I had with the nurse when I went back to the hospital, the position of the bed, the tilt of the monitor, the unending what-if that kept rotating through my thoughts . . .

I especially couldn't forget how the nurse asked me if I'd seen any white lights or experienced a tunnel during my "gone" time.

"Why? Did I say something that might have led you to believe I did?" (Okay, now it was really getting exciting!)

She looked thoughtful for a moment, then shook her head. "The only thing I recall you saying was really a question."

"Oh?"

"When we were finally wheeling you up to the step-down unit in ICU, you opened your eyes and asked, 'Can I have something to eat now?'"

I told my husband, "You should have known right then that I was ba-ack!" This is of course why some of us are fluffier than others: even when we've been dead for a spell, even when we have no memory, we know when we have missed a meal!

❖ ❀ ❖

I strongly encourage you to take a moment here to think about your own wakefulness. Give your MP a hearty gander. Have you raced by any big events in your life, ones that you need to stop and honor? Might you need to finally cry or scream? Pray or confess? Give thanks or meditate upon their hidden messages? The thing about acting like they didn't happen is that one day, at the most inopportune moment and when you least expect it, the growing impact of it will freak you out, or cause you to say no to something that should be a yes, or make you ill, or create a lump in your throat you cannot dislodge. There will likely be that final-straw incident that drives you over the edge! But not until that very moment will you realize what a big wad of overdue processing you have to grind through. So the time to take note of those biggies is now, before they implode and rob you of your zest and resilience. Wake up to them. Jot them down. Allow them to live in front of you again, admit that yes, this, too, was, and is, a part of my story, my life, of who I am today. Make peace with them, then say, "Look how far I've come!"

Or maybe you will finally admit something like, it's *true:* I *miss* my friend. I need a replacement for that person with whom I can do lunch or join for a quick round of golf after work. Maybe acknowledging that blank space will encourage you to reach out, to talk to that person sitting next to you at your son's ball game, to ask God to send you a new friend and to make him or her obvious. Maybe you'll be inspired to invite the new person in your book club for a cup of coffee or take a community college class in order to find people with like interests.

If there *is* a gaping hole in your life, *wake up* so you can become open to creative ways to fill it. WAKE UP! Life here on Earth is too short to give it away to happenstance, to hide it, to walk around sleeping or all pinched up while you wait for somebody else to serve up your joy. Maybe you almost died or lost a love you have not grieved. Maybe you never took time to celebrate your last raise or your youngest child's breakthrough. *Wake up* to what you've missed, ignored, or don't ever want to forget.

Wake up to the value of each moment you are living, for it will never come again. Only wakefulness can fill your MP pages. You don't want to get on "down the road," as my dad used to say, and discover you have a bunch of blank pages where your richest memories should reside.

3 ❋ crowned princesses of sparkledom
Friends, Fellowships, Foundations

I f we closely examine our favorite childhood memories, what might we learn about our true selves? What natural inclinations, joyful attributes, freeing tendencies, or critical tools might we have surrendered or lost along the way? How might we understand ourselves better if we discovered what *really* made us tick, way back when we could simply tick away at play?

If the tick-tock clock of your spontaneity and contentment feels like it has wound down since the days of your youth, I suggest you rewind yourself back to the past, back before you needed to "become" somebody. Join me now as I take a quick backward jaunt. Don't forget, you're playing along with your own memories here.

✳❁✳

L ong before the trademarked Slip 'n Slide was invented, me and Eenie (pipe down, ye English teachers! I like the "sound" of us—me and Eenie—and this is how I've *always* referred to us two pals!) used to lay a giant sheet of plastic down my front-yard hill, put the hose down at the top of it, and instruct our imaginary camera crew to film our brilliant commercials. I would slide on my belly, my side, or my back while pretending I had a bar of soap or perfume or whatever in my hands. Of course I always came to the perfect stop at the bottom, right in front of the camera for that close-up, where I spontaneously invented the tagline that would make people *crazy* to run to the store and buy my whatever. And now, whether I'm speaking or writing (fiction or nonfiction), I'm *still* selling, but it turns out I sell a message that I believe in enough to dedicate my "accidental" career to it: *Don't Miss Your Life!*

Several years ago me and Eenie met up in Florida after a long time of apartness. We spent the evening talking a hundred miles per hour, laughing, crying, sharing, eating snow-crab legs, butter dripping to our elbows, *mmmmmm* . . . One of the things we talked about was our parents, all now deceased, and the lasting effects they had on us. Eenie especially adored my mom. [MOMENT OF TRUTH: Some kids were intimidated by my dad, although *I* could never understand why.] Eenie lived catty-corner from us on our rural road. One of eight siblings (I have only one brother), she enjoyed coming over to comparative peacefulness, our always open candy drawer, and the ability to relax in one of our two bathrooms as long as she wanted without someone banging on the door. Her family had only one bathroom and a temperamental well; she was therefore occasionally known to bathe at our home before a date. But during our Florida meetup, Eenie told me that when she used to run across the street to visit, whether I was home or not, one of her favorite things was to sit and talk with my mom.

Eenie said she remembered my mom once sharing a concern with her (not a worry, just a bump-and-go *hmm*) about how much time I spent alone in the barn. Until that moment during our adult getaway, I'd never been aware my mother had even considered this! But it immediately crystallized to me that even way back then, I needed my space. No matter how "out there" and "alive" I am in groups, I've *always* been fed as an introvert, which somehow felt very affirming. Of course what Mom didn't know was that I wasn't really alone: my horse was a good listener and so were all my imaginative imaginary [*sic*] friends. I've *always* been entertaining in my own head, and sometimes the outside world feels like such an intrusion. (Nothing personal, dear.) Eenie's recollection from our childhood affirmed a piece of why I'm a relatively content adult today—when I get enough time alone, of course. No wonder I'm happy in the solitude of my writing labors.

I don't know who selected the line that appeared next to my picture in my senior high yearbook. The identities of those who imparted those taglines were kept top secret since some of them were kinda rude. But mine said, "I would rather sit on a pumpkin and have it all to myself than to be crowded on a velvet cushion." Not until I was in my forties and read *Walden* by Henry David Thoreau did I discover a couple things: (a) the line was quoted from a famous book, and (b) it *wasn't* a slam, which I'd always assumed. (Just *wait* till you get to the chapter on *assumptions*!) Rather it was culled from someone's innate ability to know me for who I really was, at least this little part of myself I'd revealed to him or her. I'm guessing it had to be another of my good high school girlfriends, since who else *knew* I spent that much time alone? The only thing I knew for sure was that it wasn't Eenie since she went to the Catholic high school.

Ask Yourself: How did you most enjoy spending your leisure time as a child? In a pack? In a corner by yourself? Do you carve out time in your adult life to make sure you get your fill of your natural fave now? Are you tactile? An acute listener? Who were the friends who knew you best? Where are they now? The Internet is a wonderful resource to track a few down and spend a little time rehashing. You'll maybe even get to know *yourself* a little better!

* ❋ *

Of all my childhood friends, Eenie holds the most intimate key. Yes, I became relatively close with a couple other girl-friends in high school (and oh, the string of boyfriends!), but by the time I met those other girls, I was already trying on a few "new and improved" *not*-mes and holding my feelings closer to the vest.

As we mature, we get better at hiding. Now, there's a thought worth a reread!

Others knew shades of me, but Eenie best knew my heart and true colors. She knew the true me who made mud pies as a teen. The real me who loved sleeping on the pigpen roof on her property. Oddly, there were no pigs, but that's what we decided to call that old shack. Me and Eenie shared occasional special get-paid-for chores like cleaning the whole bottom of our barn—cobwebs, stalls, storage area, and all. We earned enough money to ride the train to Chicago (a *big* deal back then!) and buy identical outfits complete with matching nail polish and pop beads! [MOMENT OF TRUTH: Two days ago I discovered a child's pop-bead set and bought it for myself, just to help me relive the glorious memory through the sound of the *pop!* as I snap them together and pull them apart, snap them together and pull them apart . . . I've had to force myself to put them down and get my fingers back to this keyboard!]

❋ ❋ ❋

When Brian, our youngest son, was growing up, he and his buddy Bob spent much of their leisure time together building forts in a woods not too far from our house. Brian served as Bob's best man at his wedding. His official best-man toast for the bride and groom spoke to the depth of his and Bob's friendship, how life changed in a good way when Cindy came along, and his joy in the couple's happiness. During the toast, Brian mentioned their childhood fort-building days and then lifted his glass so we could all toast the "ultimate fort" Bob and Cindy were readying to build together. [MOMENT OF TRUTH: I cried when I heard those romantic words from my son's lips; I cry again now typing them.] There couldn't have been a more appropriate toast, and indeed, Bob and Cindy's fort is made out of the sturdy loving stuff not even a pack of wolves could huff and puff down today. Brian and Bob *still* remain friends, both of them very engaged daddies. However, my guess is they won't tell their kids many of the childhood escapades they reminisce about—same as I wouldn't even think about sharing some of the things Eenie and me recall!

Through knowing, we know. Through being known, we learn to know ourselves.

Ask Yourself: If your best friend made a toast to your greatest asset, what would it be? What would he or she say?

What do you *wish* he or she would say?

Does your quiet strength counterbalance her flightiness? Does your impulsiveness help open him to new ideas? Do you always know how to express what others are only thinking? Are you the prayer warrior who covers her back when she's in need of defense?

Were you the naturally courageous one among your band of friends during your youth and now find yourself hesitant about everything? What happened there? Explore it with a confidant.

Are you stuck in a job that feels more like a life's sentence? How did you get there? Where were the choices? Where are they now? Speak with a friend about ways you might grow (or leap) yourself out of it.

❋ ❋ ❋

I loved playing dress-up with my kindergarten friend Nancy. My mom bought tons of fabulous lady clothes at a rummage sale and put them in a box in our basement. Nancy most often staked her claim to a blue beaded number. It was very tailored, so not for me. Over time she tried everything else in the box, too. I adored dressing up—in the same dress every single time. It had a black velvet top, cap sleeves, and, most important, yards and yards of cream-colored satin fabric. I would don that dress and twirl and twirl until it was full billow, at which point I tucked in on myself, squatted down, and remained still as a post while I allowed the soft cloud to deflate and gently skim across my cheeks and arms as I wallowed in the sensations. (Goose bumps here just remembering!) Nancy and I also raided our mom's scarf drawers and fashioned colorful costumes with our bounty. Oh, we were quite the exotic pair of dancers!

After further examination (don't forget, you're playing along with *your* own stories here), I realize it wasn't playing dress-up that I liked; it was the sensation of the twirly skirt, the flare, the billow, the satin against my skin, the swish of the scarves kicking up against the back of my calves. I was, and still am, a Gypsy at heart—and look how I've traveled the country! I am a tactile person who needs to touch things, feel the grain of the wood, the silky softness of my dog's ears, the familiar keypads beneath my fingertips. I still love to twirl and have been known to do so onstage. To this day, I am not a clotheshorse; I am pretty much missing the lady gene that's supposed to like shopping. My favorite things, which I usually find by accident, always swish, dangle, or burst with color. I wear them until they completely fall apart. I remember a woman coming to my book table after a speaking engagement and saying, "I think this is the seventh time I've seen you, and I've loved you just as much every time!" Of course I was blessed to my toes, but here's what I fretted about: it's possible I wore the same dress each time, although she was kind enough to say she didn't remember.

Ask Yourself: When I more closely examine my favorite childhood memories, what sensory things do I know to be true about myself?

What was I happiest pretending to be? An artist? *Maybe you need to take a class now.* Superhero? *What about volunteering for the Big Brother, Big Sister program, or becoming an EMT, joining the Salvation Army, or getting a part-time job as a crossing guard?* Doctor or nurse? *Have you taken CRP?* Doris Day? *Sorry, already taken.*

❊ ❊ ❊

My friend Mary and I share a long history. We met when she and Hugh moved in across the street. At that time our youngest sons were at the height of their Big Wheel craze. We had a gravel driveway that sloped down into our garage and Mary's driveway was blacktopped, so we naturally spent the majority of our time getting to know each other that summer while sitting side by side in lawn chairs on her porch—that is, between interrupted sentences during which one of us yelled at a careening Big Wheeler, "I TOLD YOU NOT TO GO BEYOND THE BUSHES!" We became each other's occasional babysitter, confidante, sanity keeper, encourager, truth teller, challenger, shoulder to cry on, and, above all, laughing partner, whether the occasion was funny or not.

One of the best things about old friends (as in long-standing friends who aren't necessarily old in your basic *codger* kind of way) is that you usually don't need to explain yourself when you get together, even if a long gap exists between meetings. If you become crabby when it's hot, they know that and either cut you slack or tell you to go to your room. The thing is, you usually don't get angry at them like you might a family member. Somehow, friends can get away with more, likely because you don't live with them. Amen.

One year, long after Mary moved to the coast, she came to my house for a leisurely stay on the way home from visiting her mom. We decided we would take a road trip to Minnesota so she could visit with Brian. Then we'd spend the night in the historic St. James Hotel in Red Wing, Minnesota, a wonderful place along the Mighty Mississip. Our trip out there was a gabfest; our visit with Brian was fun. After we checked into the St. James, we took a stroll to the five-and-dime across the street. *Oh!* The memories this place resurrected were a true blast from our childhood pasts. Worn wooden floors, parakeets, sewing notions, hardware, refill picture packs for your wallet, dollar grab-bag gifts (my mom always bought one of those when she came across them!), candy . . . you name it and this place had it.

As we sauntered down the craft aisle, through the course of conversation we discovered we both wanted to learn to do beadwork.

Back in the prime of our neighborly days, not only were we full-time moms, but we were crafters extraordinaire. With kids now grown and careers filling in the gaps, it had been a long while since either of us sank ourselves into a craft project. Hey, what better time than now, we decided, since, "Look! They have *beads*!" (See us crowding in on them, hear all the ooing and aahing.)

But whoops! "See if *you* can back off far enough to bring those teensy glass things into focus." Hear the laughter as we shared this proof-of-aging moment. Since we had just one night to-gether, we wanted to *play*, not stress ourselves out. We decided, in an unstoppable rolling ball of enthusiasm and inspiration, that we would each buy a couple packets of our favorite colors of plastic beads, which were manufactured for kids' projects but which we could see without torment. They were about as big as peas and had holes the size of straws. And what a good *idea* we came up with: string them on pipe cleaners, which would be easy! We also decided to add a buck grab bag each to our cache, go back to our room, put on our jammies, and . . . make crowns. First we set some ground rules. We could use all our beads and pipe clean-ers or just some of them. We could use anything in our grab bag. We could not look at what the other was doing until we were both done. AND (hear us giggling; see us firing our imaginations until they are glowing hot!) if we wanted to, and if we had enough mate-rials after we made our crowns, we could make magic wands, too. Mary—of *course*—immediately decided she would make a scepter, since she's more controlling. Me? I was—and still am—all about the magic. We have always been opposites. Always.

But the best part: after we don our crowns, we shall automati-cally become the Crowned Princesses of Sparkledom, a title we spontaneously invented.

Laughter. Busy hands reminiscent of previous episodes in our lives. "Olden days" conversation. New dreams shared. Creativity bursting at the seams. And then finally, *ta-da*, the Crowned Princesses of Sparkledom toasted their beatific selves!

Magic.

A treasured memory shared with a treasured friend.

Years later, Mary and I met up in California, where we again spent the night in a hotel. We brought our crowns along (gotta!), then spontaneously decided to play dress-up with them. We determined we could use anything in our suitcases, which included a bunch of my Gypsy-like clothes and jewelry I'd brought along for the business portion of my extended trip. Plus, we'd also attended a craft fair earlier in the day where I (Mary would never do such a thing) had my face painted, which looked so fun, and indeed was. If you have access to the Internet, *please* go to www.dontmissyourlifebook.com and check *these* pictures out! We are stunning. We are smiling. We are exotic! (Shades of my kindergarten scarf days with Nancy.)

We are friends.

Shortly after this picture was taken, same as before, the crowns began itching our heads, as did the face paint start itching my face. So off they came, and back to our "normal" selves we went. But the memories will never be erased. Never.

As it turns out, there's something we share that's better than our royalty status in the land of Sparkledom: we are both heirs to God's kingdom (James 2:5). Now that is royal, indeed. No itchy crowns necessary.

❊ ❊ ❊

I've shared our Princesses of Sparkledom story from the podium many times. Afterward I've received pictures of other friends—sometimes groups of friends—who heard me and decided to join our Crowned Princesses of Sparkledom Club, each shot accompanied by words of joy, fun, and memories, immediately locked up in MPs, created by the makers of *their* crowns. Although I haven't heard from any Sparkledom *guys* yet, perhaps y'all could come up with your own manly version. Hmm. What might that be? E-mail me, okay? The best I can come up with is the Crowned Princes—sans the making of the crowns, of course— of La-Z-Boys or Power Tools (hey, maybe crowns made out of wrenches?) or *Monday Night Football.* But I bet you could come up with something more fun than that!

Okay, I'm obsessing about this now, so between paragraphs I sought big George's opinion; after all, he heard the Crowned Princesses of Sparkledom story right after it took place and then later from the back of the room during a speaking engagement. And, he's a guy. "What would the male version of this be?" I asked.

His first response: "I don't get what you're getting at." Right, Mr. Engineer. So I recircled the verbal wagons, refreshed his memory about the story, redrew the concept, and then waited.

"Maybe we'd be musclemen. Or just cool guys. Or chick magnets."

"Would you have crowns?" Hear George giggling, which is cute coming from George. I adore it when George giggles. Then I hear a brief moment of thoughtful silence followed by "Maybe mustaches."

So whaddayathink, guys? Did he get it right? *Please* e-mail and let me know. My curiosity is killing me. And should the Crowned Princess of Sparkledom one day get wind of the "maybe" Mustachioed Chick Magnets, how could we resist?!

Ask Yourself: Who can you and *your* current friends become that you could not imagine becoming without them? Business

Don't miss Your life!

partners? Prayer partners? Princes of Mustaches? (For guys, I mean, unless you need an upper-lip wax job.) Supercool moms? If you can't think of anything, do you think you might need a new friend or two?

❊❋❊

After I presented a workshop called the Secret Garden of Friendship, a woman came up to me and said, "I just have to tell *you* a story." Well, of course! I *love* stories. Talk to me! She said that years ago her best friend moved away and the loss was devastating. Not that they didn't keep in contact via long-distance means, but it wasn't the same as being able to run across the street or do lunch together. She finally realized she needed a local replacement (the old friend could never be replaced, but the daily void could), so she started praying for God to send her a new friend. For what seemed like a very long time, nothing happened; her prayers grew more fervent.

During this time, however, it seemed that wherever she went, a very annoying woman showed up and sat next to her on the bleachers at their kids' events or cornered her in the grocery store. This woman made her nuts. And so she continued hounding God. *Where* is my new friend?! She feared that if this annoying woman didn't stop shadowing her, nobody would want to be her friend since they'd think, *Oh, not* her! *She hangs around with that annoying woman!*

On she prayed. She even added this to her prayers: "If *she* is your idea of replacement, Lord, she is *not* what *I* have in *mind*!"

Then one day Annoying Woman (AW) sat down next to her—again. The teller of the story said she just wanted to tell her to *go . . . away.* AW prattled on about this and that while My Story Teller (MST) tried to block her out, but to no avail. However, *one* thing AW said *did* strike a coincidental familiar chord. Begrudgingly, MST responded with her own little tidbit. And then they swapped another story, and then another.

MST: "That woman went on to become my best friend, for the last seven years now. I can't imagine my life without her!" She beamed from ear to ear during the wrap-up.

Moral of the story (as presented by MST and me): If you are lacking in the friendship department, pray, then don't assume you know what kind of person God will send you, such as how old she'll be, what religion he follows, which political party she leans toward. If all of your friends agree with your stand on things, how will you ever test your mettle on your opinions and assumptions? Just keep watching, listening, and staying open to the possibilities. Be brave enough to share some of your stories and patient enough to listen to the stories of those around you. Somewhere in the mix of the words might just be the seed that falls into your heart, takes root there, and grows a new friend. Perhaps he or she will become the friend who will help you come home to yourself again, should you be lost.

4 * humor hogties

Overcoming a Spiritually Constipated Life

One day the United States Postal Service delivers a brief life-altering letter of inquiry to my mailbox. An acquisitions editor for a book publisher has seen my work in magazines and newspapers and wants to know if I am interested in writing a book. If so, I should give him a call. Had his stunning letter arrived anytime other than when it did, I might have said no. I am neither prepared nor passionate enough about anything to fill all the pages in a book. But due to God's perfect timing, when the letter arrives our "baby" has just, three weeks previous, gone off to college. Never have I been more aware of how quickly time passes. I am all but bursting to let everyone know they should not miss their kids, since, by the grace of God, I have not missed mine. I cannot imagine living in this empty-nest period if I had.

I phone the editor and a lunch date is set. The moment I hang up, I hurl myself into freak-out mode. What should I wear to a lunch date with this respected businessman whom I don't know? If I wear my everyday mongo-size earrings, will that look unprofessional? Will my mouth even work if I don't wear a pair of my signature swinging and swaying ear bobbles with which my mouth keeps time? Since for so long I've been a stay-at-home mom, I have no idea what type of clothing suits such a *professional* meeting, so I call a few working friends to gather opinions ("Lean on me, when you need a friend . . ." Hear the music?), Moderation in clothing with my normal accessories is the consensus, so I go shopping for something between my everyday jeans and my Sunday best. Most important, "Just be yourself, Charlene. Oh, and whatever you do, *maintain eye contact,*" which is the big message of the era. Sounds simple enough, until one woman tells me how highly this gentleman is regarded, how respected he is for his theology.

Theology. I'm not even sure what the word really even means! *What was I thinking?!*

Nonetheless (and since I have more guts than brains), I arrive at the vestibule of the restaurant where we are to meet wearing my new two-piece denim outfit (stylish skirt and top), my big earrings, and a tight throat. While we are waiting to be seated, all I can think about is what I can order that won't dribble. No sauces. No gravies. No tomatoes on a sandwich that might squirt out sideways. I decide I'll check the menu and order something I can cut into little tiny pieces to parcel into my mouth while *maintaining eye contact.*

The gentleman turns out to be extremely friendly and easy to chat with. Once I get over myself and relax, things are going well. After several dainty bites, I pick up my glass of diet cola, *maintain eye contact* (he is fascinating and fun, so this isn't hard to do, still

I strive to make sure I maintain a professional persona), part my lips to grab the straw, then close them on . . . air . . . *maintain eye contact* . . . move lips to the right, open and close on . . . air . . . *stay connected with him* . . . move lips to left, open, close, air . . . at which point I glance down, and, to my horror, notice that there is no straw in my glass. I calmly set the glass down and pretend nothing has transpired. Nothing.

Since I'm also a journalist and have conducted many interviews, I find myself head-hopping, as in, now I'm in his head thinking, *What?! She seemed so perfectly normal, up until . . . what was that? Her Don Knotts puffer-fish imitation?* I cringe inside myself, then go on eating. But after a while, my thirst gets the best of me. So, *maintaining eye contact*, I pick up the glass. You can fool me once, but not twice, so I tilt the glass to my lips—forgetting that after the last embarrassing moment I *put* the straw in the glass, which, and I am not exaggerating, goes up my right nostril. This is not only embarrassing, but it makes my eyes water. Do you *know* how sensitive the inside of a nostril is? But wait, there's something worse: I am terrorized by what might happen during the straw extraction, which I quickly and deftly perform, left palm cupped over the scene of the crime. Thank goodness the straw is all that comes out!

At this point I set my glass down again and look (believe it or not, somehow I have lost eye contact) at the man who wants to know if I want to write a book. It's obvious he's trying to act like he has not just witnessed a travesty against humankind.

I have a choice here. Well, a few of them. I can flee the restaurant—and a book-writing opportunity—before I do something even worse. I can stay and try to explain that *honestly!* I *am* sane and normal. Or I can bust out laughing at my own preposterous self since I cannot simply ignore this incident. Because my parents did a wonderful job of modeling how life-giving and affirming it is to laugh at ourselves, and since I can't help myself because I also have less self-control than brains, I *burst* into laughter. When I finally catch my breath, I share with him the play-by-play of everything that has gone on in my head.

My ability to laugh at myself freed him to laugh along with me.

I've always believed this liberating incident set the stage for my first book deal, which was *Don't Miss Your Kids!* "This is who I really am," I told the businessman, who miraculously didn't bail in the middle of the luncheon, "so this is the kind of book I will no doubt write," and somehow that seemed to please him. Once you have, through the lively art and grace of laughing at yourself, gotten over fretting, you are free to just be, and look what can happen!

Humor *begins* with the ability to laugh at yourself. Of this I am convinced.

God is a comedian playing to an

audience too afraid to laugh.

VOLTAIRE

Humor is a gift from God. I am so emphatic and verbal about this that I was once asked to deliver a talk on WBEZ, Chicago Public Radio. My topic? "I am created in God's image: therefore I laugh." I mean, if "I am created in God's image" is true (and I believe it is), then if I laugh, therefore so must God. Plus, I don't think I could believe in a God who didn't have a sense of humor. I sometimes think God invented *me* just so he'd have something to laugh about! Yes, I often feel like God's one-woman entertainment show. Many times throughout my writing career, I've been asked where I get my humorous material, to which I respond, "I just wake up and follow me around." For instance, while I was in the WBEZ studio on Navy Pier in Chicago recording my segment on God and a sense of humor, a giant boom crane smashed the bumper and right-rear-quarter panel of my parked car, which was the *only* car in the legally parked area. You can see the humor in that, can't you? A BOOM CRANE! HAHAHAHA! Is God funny or *what*?!

✻✾✻

Think about it: nobody teaches us how to laugh after we pop into this world. One day we just do, and everyone who's been goo-goo and gah-gahing over us delights in our laughter. A baby's giggles bathe us in the hope that we and the child will each live happily ever after. *Our* laughing response to their marvelous, miraculous giggles is oh, *so* satisfying. By the same token, laughter in the midst of stress keeps our heads from blowing off, same with our tears. Yes, laughter is a life-sustaining, sanity-saving gift. We are born with the capacity, in great shaking gusts of God-ordained breath, to exhale it into the world.

But then . . . then what happens to wring humor out of us? All too soon we become stoic, self-possessed, embarrassed, and humiliated. We strive to cover our foibles rather than using them as springboards to laughter and therefore freedom. Feel your life shrinking just thinking about it? Our *spiritual* lives suffer from this type of emotional constipation and we feel all plugged up. *Why has all my laughter stopped?* we wonder. Where is our joy?

Rather than talking about how to "get funny," as in "I'm going to pound a sense of humor into you, and I mean it!" I'm instead going to approach the sanity of a sense of humor from the standpoint of issues that rob our natural humor-filled bent. After all, we were once laughing babies, remember? Rebel that I am, I shall do this by herewith presenting a list of my Not Even Ten (only Nine) Humor Hogties. Help for the humor-impaired, you might say. I'm intimately familiar with these hogties: like a pig is rendered helpless when a farmer ties all four of its feet together, so, too, have I felt the complete disablement of my energy and positive life force when one of these hogties hogties my humor. The following humor *dis*assembling blocks are extracted straight from my MP. Thankfully, my prolific sense of humor and parental examples freed me from their life-robbing demise so I could move on, regain my balance—and, since I am human, occasionally redo the cycle. *Sigh*. The order in which I'll present them is not necessarily indicative of their importance.

Yes, together we're tackling the topic of humor, but the sum total of these hogties is more than it appears. (I'll further shore up some of the concepts later in the book.) Consider the overcoming of these hogties as a fundamental life-enhancing skill. Without humor, we are doomed.

Humor Hogtie #1: Da-Do, Run, Run, Run

When we get too busy and frazzled, we become pinched up and hurry-scurry blind to the lighter side. Something that might otherwise be funny is simply annoying.

"Since you look like you need a good laugh, let me tell you the *funniest* thing that happened today!"

"Sorry, I don't have time for that."

I once experienced this exact phenomenon when checking into a hotel. Due to a backup of responsibilities due to an overbooked calendar due to lack of planning, all followed by a lengthy drive and a kick-and-drag luggage maneuver to get my stuff inside the hotel lobby to the check-in counter, I found myself needing to pull off a quick clothing change in order to get to a preconference meeting in a short amount of time. (*Whew!* That sentence is a fine example of the pace of my life at that time.) When I stepped up to the desk, the two ladies working were chatting with each other. One of them was sharing a funny story, one she apparently didn't want to interrupt. She drew me into their private circle (so she thought) by talking louder and flicking her eyes back and forth from me to her coworker so I wouldn't miss the details. I'm sure I looked like I needed a chuckle, too, which I did.

But the clock was ticking. As much as I *needed* a good laugh, I kept my ears slammed closed. I continued to look at my watch and clear my throat several times, even though both women had made eye contact with me. I considered not pounding but pulverizing the bell there on the counter.

Finally my mouth opened and out came "Could you please check me in!" [MOMENT OF TRUTH: There was not a hint of civility in my voice.]

Normally I love a good story. Normally I want to hug the people who make me laugh. But I wasn't about to give this woman a chance. True, her semi-ignoring behavior wasn't professional, but neither was mine. I was rude. Even though they did see me, I could have immediately expressed my time line, after which I'm sure we would have all moved right along. Instead, my own silence sank me into victimhood. (If you are *often* prone to feeling like a victim, reread that recap.)

I could have kept a more thoughtful calendar, since that was the real seedbed that grew my inability to enjoy a good laugh—which is what I'm sure I missed, since after I walked away, I heard the woman say, "So let me quick tell you the rest." She was done in about two sentences. Their roaring laughter chased me all the way down the hall to my room.

I once heard a speaker say, "If the devil can't make you sin, he'll make you busy." Watch for the smoke trails.

How About It? If you are overbooked, whose fault is it? Seriously, whose fault? Who signed you up for all those things, *agreed* to take on more responsibilities at work, let the kids be five-sporters each, volunteered to help someone when *you* should be asking for help? Remember: because we have a finite amount of hours in a day, every yes to one thing likely renders a no to something else. Don't let that be your sense of humor!

Then again, maybe learning to say *N-O is* your solution to over-booking.

Humor Hogtie #2: The Pause That Refreshes and Refuels

When the gas tanks on our vehicles run low, we refuel them. Why aren't we that smart with ourselves? Why is it we can recognize when another's laughometer runs low, but we can't detect when the needle on our own snicker scale no longer even registers?

Case in point: today's parents are inclined to use a time-out chair when their children are over the edge. The parent sees the child needs a time-out; the child gets one. But what about you? What do you do, or stop doing, when *you* need a time-out? It's true that some periods in our lives seem to allow for more time-out opportunity than others, but when do we need them more than when we are crazed?

The reality is this: all times in our lives permit at least a two-minute breather. I know this. I preach this. But when I forgot it . . .

And here's the thing, we are God's children, and God is watching us, no doubt many times thinking, *Now, that's a time-out, child of mine*. However, God never sends us "over there" to implement a punishment or cooldown period, but instead he calls us to a holy rest. God calls us unto himself. *Come to me, all you who are weary and heavy laden and I will give you rest.* Notice that says *all*, not just those of you who have your act together, or who offer the most eloquent prayers, or give the most to your church or favorite charity, or won the championship game, or closed the deal, or never made a mistake, lost your temper, or let someone down. God calls *all*.

I picture God smiling, tapping his knee, and saying, "Come, child of mine. Come here to my lap for your time-out. With me. Let me hold you. Let me love you. Let me restore you."

"But, God, you don't know how busy I am."

"Oh, but I do, which is why you need to stop for a moment."

"But, Lord, you don't know what a wretch I've been."

"But I love you."

"If you knew what I did five years ago . . ."

"I do. Come. Sit. *Sssssssh.* I love you."

❊ ❊ ❊

Once after I presented the above time-out scenarios at a speaking engagement, a woman waited until the rush at my book table was over, then approached me with tears in her eyes. She said she was so glad I was telling that story. She said she was a time-out chair mother whose rascally son had spent lots of time in his time-out chair. Then one day a terminal illness had infiltrated his little body; shortly thereafter he had died. "If I could do it over," she softly said, "I would have spent more time in that chair with him." She loved the image of God calling us to his time-out lap and said she was going to climb into it herself when she got home.

❋❋❋

My dad loved to laugh and he loved to make people laugh. When it came to solving tool-and-die and metal-stamping-design problems, he was often referred to as an expert. As the owner of his own business, he had responsibilities galore. Plus, he was a very present and engaged father.

Was he perfect? Of course not! But Dad was a genius at something: knowing when he needed to step away from a problem, especially one that didn't have an easy solution. He knew how to shake off the pace. I worked for my dad for several years, so I got to see this gift in action not only at home, but especially at work. Sometimes when business matters were the most chaotic and pressure laden or a solution was not easy coming, that's when dad would decide— as in a twinkle flash he would decide—to play eighteen holes of golf or go fishing. Just like that. "I'll be back," he would announce. Dad trusted his process. After he'd been out in the fresh air, allowing his subconscious to roam free while he engaged in something else, back he'd come looking all the happier for the wear—and with resolutions! And somehow, all the work managed to get done. He was also a hunter and a bowler and he raced harness horses as a hobby. (Yes, I was a racetrack brat and loved every minute of it.) Dad was a live-life-large and *balanced* kind of guy. Now, that *is* genius and no doubt one of the best keys to *his* bountiful laughter.

I still miss you, Dad. Thank you, Dad.

How About It? When was the last time you stared into space? When did you last blow bubbles (ah, all that deep breathing) or meditate upon a scripture verse or favorite quote for days on end by Post-it noting it above the kitchen sink, inside your wallet, near the handle on the toilet, and/or on your steering wheel?

Humor Hogtie #3: Simon Says—or Does He?

Here's an odd thing: sometimes we mindlessly kill our own sense of humor because we simply don't give ourselves *permission* to play or laugh.

—"I yelled at my wife this morning. I don't deserve to laugh." Hmm. Perhaps you just need to apologize, which extracts the guilt cork that plugs the bottle of humor. "But I won't see her until tonight after work." To which I say, *choose* apology—*commit* to apology. Commit to make it right, and vow to find a funny "I'm sorry" card on your way home. While you're looking at the funny cards you'll probably find your own laughter again, which will make your face much more pleasant to look at than that stormy one you left behind. And with your happy face, an apology on your lips, and a funny card in your hand, pucker up, bucko!

—"I have a giant zit on the end of my nose. I simply cannot draw attention to myself by letting my hee-haw snorting laughter escape." Zit on the end of your nose! HAHAHAHAHHA! I had to present to six hundred ladies with one of those. It was the first thing I talked about. Laugh? We all cracked up! Who hasn't had one of those?

—"I am not worthy." That's sure not God's opinion, so why is it yours? Do you think God wants to look at that crabby face?

—"Back to the zit scenario, Charlene. Didn't you notice that I snort when I laugh? It's humiliating." Peals of laughter. The lilt of laughter. Belly laughs. Snorting laughs. They're all proof that humankind has not lost its beautiful music. I'd take a snort-a-licious melody over a stifling silence any day! To judge the nature of someone's laugh, especially when you're doing it *yourself*, is a crime against your uniqueness.

—*But I've lost my father, and funeral arrangements are not funny,* thought I, when along with my sons I had to identify my beloved father's body and meet with the funeral director to make arrangements. It felt like all the laughter in my body shriveled up and died when I stood looking at my dad's beloved hands that had wrapped around mine, hugged me, taught me to bowl, hunt, golf, fish, build a horse stall, hang on tightly to the reins of horses and life and love.

When we got back into the funeral director's office (and honestly, I do not remember taking those steps away from Dad's body), he began going over a checklist. At some point I mentioned how shocking it was to have the "routine" implantation of a pacemaker followed shortly thereafter by my father's death.

"A *pacemaker*? Your father has a PACEMAKER?" Suddenly the soothing, near-whispering voice of the funeral director was high-pitched and bordered on panic.

"Yes . . ."

"This is important information!" He flipped through a few pages of documents and began furiously scribbling on one of them. Upon completing this task, he seemed to settle himself down, after which he spoke more normally. "During cremation, a pacemaker can explode."

Explode! Yikes! My dad could *explode*! Not funny. And yet I began to feel a great burst of laughter rising up in my throat. It's as though my dad nudged me in the arm and said, "Why hold back!" Suddenly, and much to the shock of funeral man and my sons, I exploded in laughter. Exploded! The more I laughed, the more I laughed. The more I laughed and laughed, the more clearly I envisioned my father coming to life just to tell everyone *this* story! Who, more than my dad, would love to go out with a bang, to have such a theatrical moment to broadcast throughout heaven? Honestly, I think he orchestrated this bizarre moment just to remind me that laughter—the hope of laughter—still lived.

Of course I laughed till I cried, bawled, sobbed . . . and then I laughed and cried some more.[1]

Grace. Healing. Stories. Laughter.

Give yourself permission.

How About It: Did any of the above scenarios ring your bell? If so, march yourself straight to the mirror, look at your lips, and give them permission at least to smile. Or have you noticed yourself *stifling* a laugh, say in church, thinking it's rude to laugh, especially when you don't want anyone to know what you think is so funny? [MOMENT OF TRUTH: Thank you, bless you, those of you who have not been able to stifle your laughter in church. You make me feel like our true selves are welcome there.]

HUMOR HOGTIE #4: SLEEPLESS IN SEATTLE, SKOKIE, AND BED

I'm snarky when I'm tired. Are you? And if you're tired right this minute, are you tired because of some trauma that can't be helped, like illness? Perhaps a clever and insightful friend bought you this book as a get-well gift! (If you have a sick friend, this is a subliminal message.) Sick tired can't be helped. We need to respect it and allow our bodies to spend their energies getting us well.

Or are you tired from lack of discipline about your own bedtime? A Web MD entry (www.webmd.com) says, "Not sleeping enough and not sleeping well is not OK. As a matter of fact, there is quite a price to pay. It may surprise you to learn that chronic sleep deprivation, for whatever reason, significantly affects your health, performance, safety, and pocketbook." Yikes! Do you need to visit the overbooked agenda again for this one?

If you're not sleeping well, perhaps you need a new mattress.

Or white noise, if you're a light sleeper, like an oscillating fan so you don't hear every creak and snore. Maybe you just need to turn off the television set and stop letting the lure of the late-night shows dictate your bedtime. Maybe if you went to bed earlier, rather than washing those four dishes in the sink, you'd wake up more refreshed. Washing them in the morning—taking time to soak your cuticles in the warm sudsy water while praying for the pace of your day, asking God to help you reclaim your humor, or meditating on that scripture or poem you put everywhere—would set a good pace for you. It's so much easier to do *anything* when you're not tired.

How About It? What about your priorities? Where, on your to-do list, is "Get enough sleep!"? Think of one small change in your evening agenda you can create to help make that happen.

HUMOR HOGTIE #5: CIRCLE OF DOOM

Perhaps you are surrounded by too many negative people and you need to recoup a little breathing space. Maybe you don't have enough lighthearted influence in your life and it's time to start praying for someone new to infiltrate your circle of doom. At the very least, rent some funny movies or watch *I Love Lucy* reruns. (Now, Fred, there's a doomsday kind of guy!) Get yourself a caller ID. When you're feeling low tide and you see that person calling—the one who needs a half hour of your time to unload the same thing she's told you for the last forty-five days straight, and it's become clear to you she doesn't do *anything* to help herself other than vent to *you*—don't answer. Let her unload to voice mail tonight, then delete the call and get too busy for that daily return call. Really, get busy doing something positive. Good friends are a bellows to the fire of waning, sanity-saving good humor. And yes, good friends take turns exchanging their bad moments and being the momentary needy one. But if you're in too many one-way *I GIVE EVERYTHING!* kinds of relationships, cut a few cords and pray about this—not necessarily in that order.

How About It? Have you ever thought about the amount of energy others—those whom you call your everyday friends—either zap or fuel you? Are you in a healthy two-way exchange with your intimate circle of friends, or is it all one-sided: theirs? When was the last time you spent time with a positive person?

HUMOR HOGTIE #6: THE YES! IN *NO*

As a natural follow-up to our last Humor Hogtie, we're going to take a moment here to talk about boundaries. There are times in my life when I can live my life outside the lines and fly, baby, *fly*! See my glorious, humor-filled self, a skywriter winging forth bright fluffy stories pointing to grace and life to the full! There are other times, however, when it's all I can do to hang on to myself and my own sanity. (Help, I can fly, I can fly! But I can't land! I can't even emit a pathetic jet stream, let alone create words with it. I am nose-diving!) There are times I'm a great prayer warrior for others, and times I'm not even a prayer putter. Daily devotionals? Been doing them for weeks. Daily devotionals? Twenty blocks in mindless cruise control. No wonder I don't feel centered.

Here's the thing about boundaries: they apply to everything in this book over which we have control. It's good to set boundaries on too much navel-gazing and too much outward looking, too much go-go-go-go and too much couch time . . . You get the idea. Under our own power and might, too much of a good thing (and especially a bad one) will zap not only your humor but your satisfaction with your life.

How do we identify those healthy boundaries? Good question, especially since we're each so different. Whereas a glass of wine or two might be okay for me (hear my laughter increasing with each sip), a sip could do you in (see your alcoholic rage consume you and everyone around you). Whereas one speaker wanders the hall looking to glean more energy from those in attendance, another hides because her reserves are empty. Whereas one gent or woman heads off on yet another fishing trip, another needs to set boundaries on the number of times he or she can trudge off with hip waders in tow since it's good to take turns staying home with the kids. ("Remember our deal, honey?") No budget boundaries? The aftermath of that havoc would cause all of us to lose our humor.

An in-depth discussion about personal boundaries is worthy of its own book. If you're struggling with limits or understanding the nature of what your own should be, get thyself to a bookstore or library, counselor or support group. Put a boundary on your extracurricular leisure reading (as in no more of it) until you read up on, and get some counseling in, coming to terms with your choices about such things. Hopefully, some of the pluck-and-play stuff in this book will help you with those choices, too.

But if you think you have *God's* boundaries figured out, keep thinking.

How About It? In what areas of your life do you feel out of control? Who or what might help you set reasonable limits?

Humor Hogtie #7: Heritage of Humorlessness

"It's lovely that you were raised in a family that liked to laugh, Charlene, but to be honest, my family did not. We attended church at least three times a week and our preacher was all fire and brimstone. I'm not certain we know the same God."

"*My* parents! They'd never laugh at someone's foibles, especially their own. They would deem that type of 'humor' rude and too much information. We were private people. And my dad was an alcoholic."

Now hear this: The past is over. You can't do a thing about it. But you *can* allow yourself to learn a new way, a lighter way, to grow alongside the humorless roots you've known. Let the lighthearted-look stories in this book bear witness to that way. Know I'm praying as I type (seriously) that God will illuminate the ones you need to hear—to *know*—and that you will have the courage to sow a whole new garden of laughter.

❊❊❊

Isaiah 43:18–19 speaks beautifully about helping us let go of the past to make way for the future. Since we are each unique and learn in different manners, I'm going to give you a few translations. Read each of them slowly. Select the one that best breathes itself into you and see if you can memorize it, thereby tucking it into your MP. Revisiting this wonderful instruction and promise on a regular basis will help you move on, but furthermore, it will encourage you to learn to live on the edge of a wonderful expectancy.

Do not cling to events of the past or dwell on what happened long ago. Watch for the new thing I am going to do. It is happening already—you can see it now! I will make a road through the wilderness and give you streams of water there. GNT

Forget the former things; do not dwell on the past. See, I am doing a new thing! Now it springs up; do you not perceive it? I am making a way in the desert and streams in the wasteland. NIV

Do not [earnestly] remember the former things; neither consider the things of old. Behold, I am doing a new thing! Now it springs forth; do you not perceive and know it and will you not give heed to it? I will even make a way in the wilderness and rivers in the desert. AMP

Forget about what's happened; don't keep going over old history. Be alert, be present. I'm about to do something brand-new. It's bursting out! Don't you see it? There it is! I'm making a road through the desert, rivers in the badlands. MSG

How About It? You don't want to be the next generation to hogtie the laughter, do you?

Humor Hogtie #8: Media-Induced Meltdowns

Missing children. Drugs. Car bombs. Stock market. Republicans. Democrats. Gasoline prices. Thinking about it is enough to keep you up all night and mentally fill in *all* your driving blocks. No wonder we don't know how we got somewhere with all of that toxic, alarming, worrisome stuff winging around in our heads.

Ongoing terrible news can stress you out, nab your energy, and enable fear to get a stronghold that claims your life's zest. What's a person to do with all of the violence, volatility, arguing, and uncertainty in the world? What's to laugh about by the end of the evening news or after the last section of the newspaper is folded and recycled? And now the headlines and business e-mails can follow you on vacation, to dinner, and into the bathroom via countless bad-news-bearing gadgets. But dare we become uninformed? Charlene, what would happen *then*?

Let's pretend for a moment that you have a twin. Your twin is staying at a fishing cabin in the middle of nowhere where his cell phone doesn't work. There is no Internet connection available to him, and the mail arrives only once a week via bush pilot.

You, meanwhile, are stationed in the media-infused life in which you're living.

Prompted by the early-morning light streaming through the blinds, your twin opens his eyes. While stretching, he hears the call of a loon. You, on the other hand, are awakened every morning at five-thirty by the voices on a talk-radio program, your alarm sound of choice. You learn there was a tragic house fire last night just two neighborhoods away in which a family of four has died. While your twin eats breakfast to Mozart, then James Taylor playing on the old cassette player he dragged along to the cabin, you spoon yogurt into your mouth with your eyes glued to CNN. More car bombs. His walk to the fishing boat is peaceful; the all-news-all-the-time channel escorts you on your drive to work. "Democrats did . . . Republicans said . . ." While your twin cooks a shore lunch (he smells the woodsy fire, the lake trout, baked beans, and potatoes with onions frying in the morning's bacon drippings left in the skillet) and listens to the crackle of the fire, you grab a sandwich at the local deli, where a TV blares in the upper-right-hand corner. The stock market is tanking. Dinner? He opens a can of whatever and so do you. He dines on the porch and reads another chapter of a classic book he found on the shelf; you dine on the porch with the evening newspaper spread out before you. Another third-world country makes headlines. Your twin fills his evening with more pages of his book and watching the sunset over the lake. He turns in. You watch *CSI* and the 10 P.M. news. Take your pick of the segments: it was all bad news. Even the weather.

Who do you think sleeps better? Feels better? Is better off for the input he receives? Who has less stress, lower cholesterol, a better sense of humor?

Let's start with cholesterol since, oddly, that's what got your attention. It's hard to say who has lower cholesterol. Your twin's got that shore-lunch-bacon-drippings thing going; you're eating yogurt. You worked out after dinner while he sat like a slug on the porch. But then there's heredity, plus you do like your steak and cottage fries. Also, they say stress can be a contributing factor in high cholesterol, so I don't feel like we have enough information to make a call.

Who do you think sleeps better? Again, we need more information since perhaps his cabin bed is lumpy and smells moldy, plus there's a hoot owl doing his thing all night and it's stationed near your twin's window. You, on the other hand, might—might—adore the new mattress you purchased after thinking about Hogtie #4 regarding more rest. But does it help you sleep?

Who feels better? Same thing. Hard to tell. Too many variables.

But who is better off for the input he receives, feels less stressed? It's possible (dare I say likely?) that even with the yogurt, new mattress, good cholesterol, exercise et al, that you feel pressed down and powerless, wrung out and humorless? Sure, he might, too, if he's at the cabin mentally working out a divorce (loons sound lonesome to him, not calming), a recent layoff, illness, or other loss over which he has no control. But still, you are the one now carrying the weight of your personal life *plus* all the media-inflamed news on your shoulders, most of which you can do absolutely nothing about. When are you presented with an opportunity to laugh, even at your own funny thoughts, when you are glued to one form of information or another—especially during a "BREAKING NEWS!" story? And have you ever noticed that when it's breaking, within forty-eight hours afterward, all of the "facts" prove to be incorrect? Why not just wait two days to tune in until somebody verifies something that actually is fact?

Oh, how much of our time we give away to gluing ourselves to the horrors of others!

✽ ❖ ✽

N ow imagine this: You change your alarm setting to a classical-
music channel, which plays in the background as you send up
prayers for all the people in the world who are in need, including
your twin who seems to be hiding. You ask God to show you one
or two places where you can make a difference, donate your funds,
or volunteer your time, then commit to keeping your ears and eyes
open for the answer as to how best to do so. For breakfast, you do
what you need to get a news fix and stay in the watercooler-conver-
sation loop, but you listen to a positive or funny CD (or MP3 music)
on your way to work. Okay, you go to the deli for lunch, but you chat
with a friend rather than keeping your eye on the TV. You catch a
radio news channel on your way home from work (if you must, although it's not really a good transition if you're trying to gear down
so you can enjoy your family when you arrive) and read the paper
before dinner. Or instead, maybe you quickly track a few Web
headlines, ones that offer varied opinions and are generated from
different countries—but not until after you have first wallowed in
the comfort of your home and family. You eat dinner in silence
or swap stories with your kids, who love to share their squirrely
moments because you've shown them how. Maybe you watch your
favorite show (one of the *CSIs*—although they're gory and tense so
at least check another channel on *occasion*), call a friend, work a
puzzle, or give the kids a bath. Then you take one yourself and go to
bed early with a good book, rather than lying down with the fresh
images of war-torn anywhere in your mind. Remember, as you nod
off praying, that God is on duty.

How might your life change after a few days of this?

All news all the time kills our perception and blinds us to the
joys and potential for laughter that surround us. You can live only

the life you have, not that of "the other," not even if he's your twin. We all have our issues to contend with. But you can turn off—or at the very least control and limit—the amount of no-good, terrible-rotten, disturbing news that enters your consciousness.

Try listening to *no* news for just one day and see if your lack of worry changes anything in the world. (Professional worriers: try not to worry about what terrible thing you might be missing.) Replace the news with prayer or play, a phone call or a live performance. Just try it and see what happens to your stress, your gut, your humor.

How About It? How much news do you take in during a day or week? Are you attentive to what happens to your breathing when you consume the news? Do you think the world would change if you didn't know about "it" until tomorrow?

HUMOR HOGTIE #9: IT'S NOT OVER TILL I *SAY* IT'S OVER!

Maybe you're *withholding* laughter by swallowing it down because "that person" you're mad at—and everyone else who knows about the debacle, the offense against your intelligence, the attack against your sensibilities, your very . . . ego—will think you're over "it," and gosh darn it, you're *not* over it. You're *not* done punishing them yet! Withholding your laughter and stifling your humor is proof positive that "that person" was *wrong. You* were *wronged*. I mean, if you went around with a lighthearted spirit, what would that teach them about their despicable actions and the effect it had on you? Huh?

So let me get this straight. There will be no joy in Selfville until you say so, right? And you say that no joy—no laughter, no kidding about something so serious, no making light of their egregious offense—helps to set the record straight. After all, if "that person" has to think about this (your nonsmiling face, which serves as an ongoing reminder of his offense) for a month or two, or maybe even another decade more, so be it. *If* she apologizes one more time, or perhaps for the first time, then—*then*—you'll allow maybe one snigger to escape your lips. But only if it's something truly funny, which means likely a joke on *him*. After which time you shall consider if having allowed said snigger to escape your lips was worth it, which, if "that person" also sniggered, it likely won't have been since he didn't *deserve* to laugh, the viper!

Did I get it right? Did you see yourself? Touch you somewhere too close to your pride? If so, I bet the obvious point of the story made you bristle, in which case you have hogtied yourself. When you "no allow the laffy" in order to punish "that person," you hogtie yourself. End of story.

✳ ❋ ✳

Yes, I know, I know. I'm talking about forgiveness here. I'm talking about forgiving a terrible offense. Perhaps just thinking about forgiveness causes your jaw to clench—unless *you* have at long last experienced the grace of receiving the tender, earnest, and life-giving words "You are forgiven" and seen the light of the truth in her eyes when she said it. She *means* it. OH! Or you can tell by the curve of his lips, the return of his dimple, that he truly does forgive you. He has surrendered his anger, which has enabled *him* to smile again, too. It's as if the woman I witnessed in the airport, the one who wanted the little boy greeting her to feel her happiness by placing his hand on her fast-beating heart, has shown your beloved how to help you feel his forgiveness by allowing *you* to see his *smile*. It's as if you've been holding your breath for a thousand years and the divine breath in his forgiving words, which floated over the curve of his lips and surged into your tight lungs, has at long last enabled you to exhale. You can breathe again.

Drink this, all of you.

This is my blood, God's new covenant

Poured out for many people

For the forgiveness

Of sins.

MATTHEW 26:27—28 MSG

If you have ever experienced forgiveness, remember *that* the next time you have the opportunity to pass it along. Withholding forgiveness is like tying your own bubbling spirit of laughter to a whipping post.

How About It? Are you waiting to forgive someone? Why? When was the last time you received the blessed relief of forgiveness—no matter how large or small your offense?

❊ ❈ ❊

I can think of no more fitting closure or stronger witness to the correct perspective on the importance of a sense of humor than this: "Anxiety is the prerequisite to humor. Human beings are not amused by the irrelevant, but by what matters. Through laughter, we diminish the burden of fear, make light of forces we cannot control, and defuse the anguish of despair."[2]

That pretty much says it all.

5 * always question your assumptions
Sometimes They're (GASP) Wrong!

Hold tight to your precious postulations before reading on because my intention is to rattle your cage enough to shake a few assumptions loose, maybe even unnerve you.

But if I don't succeed, would that be a bad thing? (Hey, if you enjoy living in la-la land, who am I to boot your buttinski out of it, right?) But if I do knock your assumptive self a tad off kilter, then what? Might I even crack your foundation? Or do you assume it's uncrackable? What if one of the upcoming stories first jackhammers your entire cement slab into smithereens and finally enables you to raise a new structure on a better foundation, one that even the big bad wolf cannot huff and puff into oblivion?

Let us find out!

A good place for us to begin our creative work …

STOP!

After reading that last partial sentence, you might have already assumed that you'll literally have to "work" your way through this chapter, like by answering questions (Hey! I just *did* that!) and going through a big self-evaluation. You might have even assumed I'll ask you to get up out of your chair to retrieve a piece of paper, or even something *more* strenuous, like draw a chart. You therefore might have already determined you're going to take a *break* from this book because you're not in the *mood* for "work," since, well, you're all about laughing now that your humor has broken free from its hogties.

Well HA! on *you* and your errant *assumptions*! You do not have to "work" in the literal sense, since most creative work turns out to be play anyway. (Read that sentence again.) In fact, I'm sure this chapter will contain a few *very* funny stories, so let the laughter continue! The only reason I used the word *work* is that many self-gains *do* take hard work. But we're all about pluck-and-play, remember, so relax and move forward. Just don't forget to stay on guard. (Sneaky, eh?)

The best place to begin our journey for a chapter on assumptions is to go back and reread Humor Hogtie #8, the one including your theoretical twin—unless you really *do* have a twin, in which case *my* assumption was incorrect, which was that I needed to dream up your twin for the sake of analogy. But I digress. The twin analogy is a great illustration for this chapter, too, since I'm guessing you kept getting caught up short in your assumptions. For instance, when I first mentioned that your twin is staying in a fishing cabin in the middle of nowhere, you assumed he was leading the life of Riley on a swell vacation, right? And do you not assume when you hear the "life of Riley" expression that at some point in time there really was some guy named Riley? That he did indeed have a grand life, even though you don't have a clue as to where that age-old expression came from? I mean, what if the generations of folks who repeat that saying—which includes the person from whom *you* first heard, then repeated it—also assumed (because *nobody* looked up the root of this Riley guy) that Riley had the good life when, in actuality, Riley's life reeked? In order to serve as a good example, I'm going to question one of *my* longtime assumptions right now and go a-Googling because I don't have a clue either. Who was this Riley guy, and why have I always assumed I want his life? Seriously, I am going to stop typing at the end of this sentence and look it up.

(*Brief pause while Charlene Googles.*)

The results are shocking! Here's what the *Dictionary of Word and Phrase Origins* by W. and M. Morris has to say:

> Whoever this guy Riley is, the tax collector would probably like to know about his source of income. People attribute such a grand lifestyle to him that he must have done quite well for himself. In fact, no one has ever traced the expression to an actual person, and he or she probably never really existed. But we do know where the expression almost certainly originated. His name was originally O'Riley (or O'Reilly—the spelling varies) and he was given life in a song, "Are You the O'Riley?" made popular in the late 19th century by the great vaudeville performer, Pat Rooney. In the song, O'Riley is always looking to strike it rich and lead the good life. Today, of course, we are more realistic about the possibilities of getting rich quick and actually living the life of Riley.

E-*gads*! Aside from the fact I've already implied that many of our life's benchmarks can be triggered through song (I love feeling so validated!), is *this* what you or your twin really want? A life based on a life that likely never existed?! [MOMENT OF TRUTH:

O'Reilly is Irish, too, so I've just claimed him as *my* imaginary twin!]

But enough about Riley; let's get back to your twin, who does or does not exist either, the one you assumed was on a swell vacation. The more questions I raised about him, the more you likely realized that things might not be as you assumed. We learned that maybe he's not vacationing after all, but that he is hiding, trying to deal with a great devastation about something like high cholesterol, lack of sleep, job loss, or a recent divorce. Watch out what you wish for (Oh, if only I could be like that guy at the fishing cabin!) since sometimes you don't have a clue what you're talking about.

Let's move on to someone whom you know to exist and you also know lots about: you. (For the sake of this story, let's assume you go to church, but even if you don't, you'll still get the drift.) How often do you notice that same woman in church every Sunday, the one who always sits in the third row on the right? She has that perfect spiritual hairdo and prays the most eloquent prayers. (I mean, she knows *every* godly key word!) Her children are always *so* well behaved during the service. (You know who I'm talking about!) If you could just be like *her*, since *she's* got her act together! Her family is never late for anything and her house is as neat as a pin. But you? To call you "slightly askew" when you come trudging in the back door halfway through the first hymn is a huge understatement. You've already had a doozy of a Sunday-morning fight with your husband, who stayed home today. (What kind of a spiritual leader is *he* compared to *her* husband, who sits there every Sunday with his arm draped around her shoulders, pulling her close to his side. He obviously *adores* her!) While her children have their hands folded in their laps, your kids are smacking each other. You're too busy to stop them since you're silently praying, *Lord, don't let our small group,* the one Ms.

Spiritual Hairdo also belongs to, *have another one of those "circle" prayers tonight where they expect everyone to pray out loud.* Please, *God! I'm always so humiliated by my bumbling words.*

Oh, how appearances invoke certain assumptions. But what if you didn't know *this* about Ms. Spiritual Hairdo: she belongs to an OCD support group. Obsessive-compulsive disorder. She cannot quiet her ongoing attempts to achieve perfection, including all but counting the hairs in her perfectly coiffed do.

Let us get into *her* head for a moment while she thinks about *you. If only I could relax like that woman who arrives late every week. See, nothing terrible happens just because she's tardy. And OH! how I wish I could pull off that wild hairdo. I bet she didn't have to get up at 4:30 A.M. to make that happen; it just naturally does. And I love her honest talks with God. I hope she takes a turn tonight if we do another prayer circle. I don't seem to know how to just be real with God, and she just . . . talks to him. Says what's on her mind. What a true friendship she and God must have rather than the one I keep striving for. Plus, what a relief it would be to leave this man behind for an hour. He's so jealous; he won't even let me come to church by myself! I can barely breathe from his nonstop suffocation and expectations . . .*

True, everything I just surmised about Ms. Spiritual Hairdo could be untrue—or not. But I hope you're beginning to see how our assumptions about everyone else's lives can leave us feeling inadequate and lonely. It would be better if we stopped assuming and talked to one another, listened to one another's stories. Nobody is perfect. We all have our insecurities. Now, if you assume *that*, you're on the right trail.

✳ ❋ ✳

But enough about you and pretend people; let's talk about *me* for a while. (I am smiling here.) I assumed a leisurely trip to the grocery store—you know, the kind where you just wander, see what's new on the market, read a few labels, and pick up a little of this and that—wouldn't rock my assumptive world. After all, I just wanted to relax. Wrong!

My slippery slide began in frozen foods. In an ongoing attempt to eat healthier, I spied a box of frozen veggie patties. The banner ad on the box read NOW WITH MORE VEGGIES. *Excuse* me? What were veggie patties previously made out of that the veggie-burger people feel a need to tout *more veggies*? Since I'm relatively new to the veggie-burger concept, I don't even know what to *assume* might explain this. Did they used to use beef fillers or something?

Then I came to the SPAM products. SPAM. Now, I "get" SPAM. I don't buy SPAM because it's healthy; I buy a can every once in a while because I like to slice it, fry it, sauté some onions, and serve it on toast with a tad of mustard and maybe some lettuce. Maybe. But on this trip, my breath caught in my throat when I noticed turkey SPAM! I actually hauled the only other person in my aisle, a complete stranger, right over and said, "Look at this!" (Honest, I dragged her straight in front of the can and pointed.) "Have you ever seen *this*?" She had not. [MOMENT OF TRUTH: She also didn't seem quite as distressed about it as I.] I'm assuming this is SPAM's answer to a healthier experience with their product, but I didn't bother to read the label. If I want SPAM, I want SPAM, not a fowled-up (hahahaha) replica. Who dreams this stuff *up*?

I'm sure I'll hear from you turkey SPAM lovers out there (I hope I *do*), and maybe even the SPAM people themselves, which would also be wonderful. In fact, go ahead and send me a case of turkey SPAM. I promise to try it and do right by it. But let me just say that in a million years I would never have assumed I'd find *SPAM* and *turkey* on the same label. [MOMENT OF TRUTH: I have no idea *what* original SPAM is made of. I don't care since it's just right. Same with Cheetos.]

On to the next aisle, where I found the scariest thing yet: the wrapper on a paper towel that claimed to "soak up life." To be honest, that's when I all but ran to the checkout counter. The last thing I need is a roll of paper towels soaking up one moment of my remaining and quickly vanishing years on this earth. The idea freaked me out! "Whoa! Don't get too close to the paper towels since they'll slurp the life out of you!" Too bad Alfred Hitchcock isn't alive to make something out of *that!*

So much for a relaxing trip to the grocery store.

Perhaps on a creepier note (you be the judge), George and I were engaged in the lively art of conversation (whereby usually I'm talking and George is nodding, acting like he's listening) when he retrieved his white, no-frills, 100 percent cotton hanky out of his back pocket. Unfolding it, he vigorously blew his nose, and let me just say that George is a *loud, hornking,* and serious nose blower.

After several good snorts, George laid out the hanky in his giant palm (wears a size-thirteen ring) and folded it right on the creases, again and again, until returning it to its perfect square. He put it in his right hand and slid it back into his pocket.

When he looked up at me, I'd become mute. My mouth was agape. I couldn't believe what I just witnessed and my face showed it.

"Is something wrong?" he asked.

"Do you *always* fold your hanky like that after you blow your nose?"

"Yes. Most of the time. Is that a problem?"

"Maybe."

"Why?"

"After twenty-five years of married life"—and now in a finger snap it's going on forty!—"I had no idea you folded your hanky back up after blowing your nose."

"So?"

"So, I'm sorry to tell you that when I'm doing laundry and find the hanky so neatly folded up like that, I assume it hasn't been used, so I simply put it back in your drawer without washing it."

It was George's turn to stand with his mouth agape. After a couple beats passed, he responded.

"No wonder I have so much trouble getting my glasses clean."[1]

Pause here a moment until you recover.

Did you notice the word *assume* in that story? My dad, who was also an aggressive, hornking [*sic*] nose blower, *wadded* his hankies before sliding them back into his pocket. Why shouldn't I assume everyone did that?

Now you know.

George, on the other hand, assumed the hankies returned to his underwear drawer were clean. Why wouldn't he?

Now you know.

This incident became the day we both quit assuming *quite* so many things about each other—especially the laundry. After we learned our assumptions were not always correct, behaviors changed: George takes all hankies out of his pockets when he puts his dirty clothes in the hamper, and I wash everything. [MOMENT OF TRUTH: Since this event, George retired and I'm still working, so he now does the laundry, which, when he took over the task, I assumed he knew how to do. Oh boy.]

Sometimes, however, we still both make incorrect assumptions about each other, as on the day I assumed that if I thought something was hysterically funny, so, therefore, would George. I was in a clothing store when I passed by a display of sweatshirts printed with these words: HEART OF GOLD BRAIN OF SPAM. *BWA-HAHAHAHAhahahaha.* Is that not relatable, or WHAT! I stood laughing until I cried and then snorted, which I don't usually do. I continued on with my shopping, but the more I thought about it (and continued to chuckle), the funnier it became. Finally, I went back and bought two of them: one for me and one for my girlfriend Mary Beth, whose young daughter was going through chemotherapy. (You should *see* that beautiful woman now! *Thank you, God, for restoring her health!*)

That night before George arrived home, I put the sweatshirt on. Who doesn't need a laugh at the end of a hard workday? George (have I mentioned that he's a retired engineer?) walked in and looked at the saying, which I proudly displayed before him, arms stretched to the sides for full effect. [MOMENT OF TRUTH: I blocked his path so he had to read it, otherwise he wouldn't have noticed.] I could hardly wait for the guffaw. Instead, he furrowed his brow and said, way too thoughtfully, "SPAM. That's the stuff in the can, right?" And that was that. He just didn't get it. Maybe you don't either. But to assume *nobody* gets it would be just plain wrong. Mary Beth laughed as hard as I did, as did most of the staff and other parents on her daughter's hospital floor. Maybe it's only funny if you "feel" it, eh?

❖ ✽ ❖

As with many of life's "jokes," what is funny to one person is an insult to another. To assume a person of any ethnic persuasion will think a "good" ethnic joke about same will strike them funny is courting disaster—unless it's your ethnicity, too, and sometimes that doesn't work either.

To assume your brand of religion is the only one God cares about—*fondly* cares about—is not only to underestimate the breadth of our creator's love for all creation but to fly sparks over the dry timbers of hate and prejudice until enough of them gather and ignite a war. To assume you *know* "the heart and faith of the enemy" without ever speaking to them, hearing their stories, reading their sacred books, watching them tuck their children in at night, or striving to understand their perspective by educating yourself rather than just listening to biased opinions is to pour fuel on the flames of war. To assume that any one television channel, newspaper, editorial, blog, or religious leader can fairly represent both sides of an issue, or even sanely vocalize truth about his own is perhaps the most dangerous of all.

Whether you lean to the right, to the left, or believe yourself to think down the dead center, to stop questioning your assumptions about political issues—to give away the freedom, the right, the *duty* to question them—is to devalue every human being whom you perceive to be, *assume* to be, on the "opposite side," the *wrong* side, of God's infinite love or tax debate.

No matter what your spiritual, political, or ethnic assumptions might be, question them. Hold them up to hard scrutiny under fair circumstances (*many* sources and resources and much prayer) rather than just clinging to your emotional, parroting, hotheaded, or "blindly follow" leadings. [MOMENT OF TRUTH: I'm preachin' *loudly* to myself here, too!]

❖ ❖ ❖

For two years in a row I attended portions of the annual Great Dakota Gathering and Homecoming [2] held in Winona, Minnesota. As stated by the Winona Dakota Unity Alliance, its mission is to "continue the reconciliation process by an alliance between Winona,

Minnesota, and the Dakota Nations. Our hope is to bridge the gap that exists with ˙educational and cultural projects mutually designed to bring both [groups] together in greater wholeness.'" Whereas in 1853 the Treaties of Mendota removed the Dakota American Indians from their ancestral land known as Wapasha Prairie (including Winona), efforts to reconcile that injustice, to heal the wounds of the generations through education and dialogue now exist.

The stories . . . *oh*, the *stories*! Historical, current, perspective laden . . . You cannot truly know the soul of another human being—another class, race, or country of people—until you hear their stories spoken sans your assumptive filters. All stories have at least two sides; it is good and right to hear the "other," to allow the surprises to shift you somewhere deep inside. At this gathering of peoples I learned the expression *Mitakuye Owas* (Mē-dta-koo-ō-yeh Ō-wa-say). Translation: "all my relatives" or "we are all related." As in *all*. Prominent leader, musician, actor, and speaker John Trudell said, "Look at all that connects us, but we continue to focus on the differences." Perhaps that's because we *assume* there are more differences than actually exist. He also asked, "Where are the theologians who speak against hate in the world?" Yes, I wondered. Where are they? Do they assume we don't want to hear that message during such "fearful" times?

How much richer—filled—might your life be if so much of your energy wasn't zapped by the growing evidence of global conflicts? No matter where you stand on the subject of war, can peace *ever* be a bad thing?

The fear of man brings a snare.

Proverbs 29:25 NASB

Errant assumptions based on lopsided facts create fear, and fear can take generations of people down. Nothing breeds fear like ignorance.

✱❋✱

We can take *ourselves* down with unexamined assumptions. I assumed that since I spoke on the topic of *Don't Miss Your Life!*, I was not at risk for burnout. After all, I delivered the *antidotes* to burnout.

And then I burned out. (More on burnout later.)

I am thankful that in the midst of my burnout, I did not first assume and then go on to live under the assumption that since I'd failed to heed my own words, I would never be, *should* never be, "preaching" or writing about this message again. But even though I am not perfect, even though I did not live according to what I preached for a pocket of time, even though I will still make tons of mistakes in my life, God still desires for me to live the rest of my life to the full, and to encourage others to do the same. And so God does for *all* of God's children—all living things—on this earth.

God created human beings;

he created them godlike,

reflecting God's nature.

He created them male and female.

God blessed them:

"Prosper! Reproduce! Fill Earth! Take charge!

Be responsible for fish in the sea and

birds in the air, for every living thing

that moves on the face of Earth."

GENESIS 1:27–28 MSG

Yes, some precepts are just worth repeating.

God created human beings to reflect God's nature, and God is love.

Mitakuye Owas. Mitakuye Owas. Mitakuye Owas.

✳❋✳

Maybe you've always assumed you cannot sing since, when you were a child, the school choir director asked you not to sing so loudly, please. *Please.* You'll never forget that humiliating incident, after which you began to mouth the words, since surely your voice was that bad. In fact, you don't even sing in the shower anymore since you've learned to swallow down the urge to let what swirls in your heart and rises in your throat belt from your lips.

But maybe that someone asked you to turn your volume down a notch because your projection was so wonderful—your voice so clear and distinctive—that you overrode the rest of the choir. For the sake of the school production, the choir needed to be heard as one voice, not your voice with the rest of them as backup. It's also possible, however, that you assume you're destined to be the next

American Idol, but in actuality, the only reason you'll make the show is that everyone will laugh at you. In either case, ask a few folks you trust to give you feedback on your assumptions. Record yourself and take a listen. But even if everyone does laugh, *sing anyway*! Sing in your car, in the shower, when you want to wish someone a happy birthday. Sing in church on Sunday morning when your heart swells with love for your God. But *sing*! Singing feels so good and comes so naturally.

Brian just sent me a picture of Bridget, our oldest grand-daughter. She is sitting on top of a giant round hay bale. Her three-year-old legs stretch in front of her and her arms are flung straight out from her shoulders. Her face is utterly beam-ing, her mouth wide open. The sky is filled with awesome chan-nels of wispy clouds, as though she, or God, or maybe both, have orchestrated heavenly streamers for her backdrop—this moment. Under the picture Brian wrote, "After I sat her up there, she just started singing. It was sweet. She was having a good time." The picture and his sentiment made my heart as happy as hers. I phoned Brian to ask *what* song had burst out of her. "She just makes up songs. It was something she made up." *I* instantly erupted in joy-filled laughter, then set the pic-ture as the background for my computer monitor. I want my MP to flip back to her moment, then mine at seeing it—*feeling* her joy—over and over and over again.

What is the song in your heart right now? If you composed the words and melody that would best represent your most recent happy entry in your MP, how might it go? Why not start singing and find out.

Yes, maybe you have to deal with the reality that you don't have the best voice in the world, but don't let that *silence* you. Hon-estly, those folks on *American Idol* who get made fun of, some who compose their own music, too, encourage me. If I'm just sitting here making fun of them and not going after my own dreams, shame on me! And shame on you, too.

Get up and sing! Sing until your heart is happy enough to go after your dreams. Perhaps you'll inspire someone else to follow theirs.

✽✿✽

I've always assumed I can't draw because, well, I'm not good at it. Then one day, desperately seeking a break from anything involving words, I signed up for an evening adult education watercolor class to be held at a local high school. I remember one of my friends (one of my artistic friends) saying, "Charlene! Watercolor is the most difficult medium to learn. You should start with acrylics or take some private lessons. Don't start with watercolor!"

"But I don't care if I'm not good. I just want to play with the paints," I told her.

I'm so glad I didn't assume that since she is an artist who actually sells her work, her opinion should overrule my desire. The truth is, *no*, I'm *not* any good at drawing; I wasn't even that good at paint by numbers. But I had an absolutely *wonderful* time in my class. The teacher was fun, lively, encouraging . . . I painted an awesome (anyone viewing it will surely find another word to describe such a . . . painting) self-portrait. I didn't even look in a mirror; I watercolored myself the way I felt that evening: smiling and donning blue-and-purple hair. [MOMENT OF TRUTH: A mirror would have revealed a salt-and-pepper blend.] In my painting, I have tremendously long curly eyelashes (closer to those of my youth), ab-fab earrings (of *course*), and my beauty mark (which occasionally acts like a mole and grows a big ol' long black hair, which I *sure* wasn't about to give myself!) is higher up my cheek in the painting than it is on my face now, before the aging process caused it to slide down my cheek. And I look so . . . ALERT! My eyes are WIDE OPEN! [MOMENT OF TRUTH: My eyes are disturbing. Since I stink at drawing, I gave myself entirely round irises rather than half ones. This is due to the fact I don't know how to draw eyelids (let alone anything else) and I kinda forgot I had them, which is why I look so . . . alert, aka disturbing, in my painting. If you dare, go to www.dontmissyour lifebook.com and check it out.]

✺ ✻ ✺

The point is this: Don't assume you shouldn't do something just because you're not good at it. Don't assume your naysayers are qualified to *be* the judge of whatever.

But neither should you assume you're the only one who's right and the rest of the world is wrong. Sometimes, it is what it is: a giant mistake.

6 * help! i've lost my lean

The Necessity of Balance

August. Illinois. Hot. I hate hot. When it's muggy and I am hot, I feel sick, whine, moan, and become crabby beyond tolerable, even to myself. Heat puts me in *tilt* mode. Although I've grown smarter about the warning signs and I make it a point to stay hydrated, back in my youth, I actually passed out from heat on a few occasions. No, my body does not like hot. Blaaaach.

And yet, I must prepare for an out-of-country speaking engagement. Although I am excited to once again have the opportunity to speak my passions, a part of me is dreading the journey because I'm heading to Cayman Brac, Cayman Islands. What kind of doofus whines about a speaking engagement on an island? Let us review: I hate hot.

I pack a pair of sandals, which I'm sure won't fit my heat-swollen feet, my makeup case with colorful concoctions that will slide down my face while I perspire, and a bathing suit I probably won't wear because I'll be hermetically sealed in an air-conditioned room when I'm not presenting to the ladies. *Dear God, please let the meeting room be air-conditioned!*

There is, however, a grace that overrides my languishing body: my son Bret is flying to Cayman Brac from Albuquerque, New Mexico. During a bit of time before and after the conference, as well as occasionally between sessions, mother and firstborn son will get to wallow in each other's company. "I bought a new travel guitar, Mom," he'd told me during a recent phone conversation. "It fits in the overhead." Even a doofus cannot remain completely hopeless and pitiful when anticipating the music of her grown son's life. Not even a whining, too-busy, frenzied, *hot* doofus.

We meet up at the airport in Florida and travel the rest of the way together, talking incessantly during and between takeoffs, landing, hugs, and back pats about some of the details of our lives. My side of the conversation is driven by work pressures entailing hard experiences, writing deadlines, and ongoing wads of paperwork. I am stressed and have been for some time. His smile continues to beam all over me while he shares bits about his work and touches briefly upon a difficult personal experience.

We arrive at the airport where . . . my giant suitcase does not. We wait in the tiny, hot, humid, un-air-conditioned airport for a *long* time until the very last items, including bicycles and furniture, are deplaned and checked by security. We are detained just short of forever while answering questions and filling out paperwork for the missing bag.

Ah, it's my first night away after a full day's journey and I have no refreshing toiletries, clean clothes, or seersucker nightie to separate me from the damp sheets, since, alas, my room air conditioner is not turned on when I arrive at the resort. (See Charlene crank that baby to the *freeze*!) I only have the sweat-and-recycled-airplane-air-laden clothes I'm wearing and my carry-on bag containing my speaking notes. There is only one plane a day to this location, so even though I'm here a day before my sessions begin, my clothes will not arrive until (I hope) tomorrow, when the ladies do. The hairs on the back of my neck would surely rise just thinking about a forever-lost bag, but they're being flattened to my skin by the raging rivers of perspiration racing down my back.

Fast-forward forty-eight hours. My suitcase did arrive with the ladies and both the meeting room and my bedroom are now air-conditioned. Like a lizard on the run, I scurry between air-conditioned rooms amid the shifting sessions, meals, and occasional downtime. Since I'm not sleeping well, I am, beyond human explanation, astounded to find I am zestfully energized for my presentations. Nothing short of God can explain it. No matter how hot I feel, occasionally spotting my son through the trees or hearing the faint notes of his guitar riding the balmy breezes works a soothing magic in my soul. I begin to recognize, then give thanks, that the island is stunningly beautiful, the retreat is spiritually fulfilling, and the food is beyond awesome. A miracle is taking place: I am barely talking about the heat. Yes, I am hot and I don't like it, but something bigger—something life-giving and more important than me being hot—is at work. [MOMENT OF TRUTH: I doubted this was humanly possible.]

During a luxurious long pocket of free time on the second day of the retreat, participants are offered the opportunity to select from a number of options like island tours, shopping expeditions, and snorkeling experiences. Bret and I decide to gallivant off on our own and rent mopeds for the rest of our stay. After all, I have owned two motorcycles, ridden horses in barrel races, and often bicycled a half mile to school when I was a girl. Bret has been a motorcycle guy all his adult life, usually owning several of them at once, taking great and wondrous cycle journeys across the United States. Rental office, paperwork, helmets (it's the law on Cayman Brac, even though tropical sun on a helmet will probably bake my brains), keys. Zip-zap, we are ready to explore!

We each get on our vehicle and start the engine, which sounds more like those of windup toys rather than the exhilarating *brmr-brmr-brmr* of a Harley. But then, *nothing* with an engine sounds as swell as the *gurr-purr* of a Harley! (Ah yes, I'm back to the rumble!) Bret leads the way, puttering to the opposite side of the street than we usually drive on, just like he is supposed to here on the island. Without hesitation, I turn up the gas (mopeds are all hand-operated, both gas and brakes) to set out for our great adventure, and away we go.

Within seconds, *seconds*, I am wobbling this way and that. In my attempt to steady myself, I turn the gas up a notch, thinking lack of speed is the problem, but instead I simply veer more quickly to the right. I have to drag my foot on the ground to keep from falling over. In my discombobulated state, without first decelerating, I squeeze the brake pedal too hard and nearly hurl myself off the bike. Just before driving into the ditch of the oncoming traffic lane, I—*THANK YOU, JESUS!*—come to an abrupt stop. Luckily, there is no traffic. It is the shortest, most humiliating ride of my life, even counting the time I got thrown over the head of a pony. A *pony*, for goodness' sake. What could be worse than that—other than nearly being thrown off a moped that I myself am operating?

Bret looks over his shoulder. Rather than finding his mom merrily zooming along behind him, he discovers I'm waaaay back, on the wrong side of the road, and half facing the wrong direction. "What are you doing, Mom?" he hollers. Clearly, I have no clue. With ease, he leans into the road and does a U-turn, puttering back to meet me. Although I am laughing on the outside, my insides are screaming. *What the heck was that, Charlene? You almost dumped yourself in the ditch! Are you so old now you can't ride a moped? A moped!* This unacceptable thought steels my determination.

Bret pulls up next to me and teasingly suggests that perhaps I should lead so he can keep an eye on me. "Don't be silly. I'm fine," I say through peals of laughter. But inside . . . inside I am thrown off my own base. Me, the wild and crazy Gypsy woman, suddenly can't seem to hold her balance long enough to make a charge on a moped!

As I gently turn up the gas to maneuver the bike back in the correct direction, I first turn the wheel too sharply, making it feel like I am folding the bike in half. Then I sit up too straight (wobble-wobble) to maneuver a less angled turn. It is the craziest sensation. *What is wrong with me?* Finally, feet straddled on the ground, I give it the slightest bit of gas and walk the bike until I am headed straight. I grit my teeth and take off again. After a few more slight bobbles, once I get moving more swiftly, I am okay. Until . . . we decide to turn off to look at an abandoned building. Same dumb thing! Ninety-degree turns are next to impossible to implement without gyrations, contortions, humiliation, and a sudden stop to keep me from peril.

Bret just grins and shakes his head, then utters encouragements. (Bless you, child of mine.) He also makes fun of himself, the big biker dude, riding a moped. "Cheesy rider," he yelps once while passing me. Comic relief is a wonderful thing when one is having a dumbness crisis. Perhaps things are perking up, though; we do make it all the way to the other end of the short island. But then, since the road dead-ends, I have to turn around. Wobble-

wobble I go, just like the old Weebles toys the boys used to play with. "Weebles wobble but they don't fall," so the Weebles jingle went. *What do dumb Weebles know about the reality of road burn?* Since there is no traffic, I decide to do circles and figure eights in the street until I find my balance, get it right. I even make Bret work a few turns as I study his every move, try to lock in on the mechanics of something I used to do naturally. I am now stiff as a board with determination. No amount of striving makes things better.

And then it hits me: I have lost my lean! I have lost my natural ability to lean into the turns. *Once you learn how to ride a bike, you'll never forget.* I've heard it a thousand times. Why, I ought to pummel the people with the contrary Weebles who utter that trite stuff! Too stiff. Too upright. Too fast. Too quick with the brakes. Trying to do too many things at once out of sheer determination and pride rather than taking it slowly, one step at a time, allowing instincts and balance to lead the way.

Later that evening, as Bret and I sit together under the starry sky listening to the sounds of the ocean lick and lap at the shore, it *really* hits me: I lost my lean not only when it comes to riding a bike. Through overbooking, too much whining, dragging too much stuff all over the place, and allowing negative thinking like *I hate heat* to blind me to awesome possibilities, I have nearly lost my lean on *life*.

Oh, sweet metaphor of life, at last I've found you!

❋❋❋

When we are awake to our lives, it is amazing how even an instant evaluation of our most recent MP entry can speak to us, tutor us, and even warn us. *Do you see how close you came to crashing and burning? You were so close to losing your lean on your life, Charlene.* When the ocean breezes blew into the deepest part of me—when my shoulders relaxed and I could inhale and exhale in peace—I could look back and read the graduating warning signs. Going into this trip, I mentioned that I'd been too busy. Sitting on an airplane on the way out there—sitting next to my son, whom I hadn't seen for a long while—rather than sharing what was good and right and beautiful about my life, I talked about how busy I've been, how "driven by work pressures entailing hard experiences, writing deadlines, and ongoing wads of paperwork." (Feel my life leaning?) I realize that for me, whining is a warning flag that I am ensnared in a self-pity feeding frenzy. I need to stop the mouth. Maybe take a nap. Play for an hour or two. Reread my own chapter on Humor Hogties! Regain my balance rather than giving precious moments away to whining about the bad ones.

And you? What are your warning signs that your life is heading toward a crash? What do you need to do to stop it?

When I experienced my first signs of trouble on the moped, I didn't stay relaxed. I started internally berating myself. More tension, more stiffness—less balance. See how that works? Rather than surrendering my ego, I steeled my determination.

Did I just hit you between the eyes with that one?

* ❋ *

I cannot literally explain why, after all these years, I'd suddenly lost my lean. Then again, *suddenly* is an interesting choice of words since perhaps I'd lost my lean decades ago. Possibly, so did you. Although there *are* things that wham-bang into our lives over which we have no control, more often than not our use of the word *suddenly* is an exaggeration. Little by little, moment by moment, we let go of attentiveness. (Reread that last sentence until you are attentive to it. Seriously, do it.) Then, when for a moment we are awake to life, we notice that things have changed. It is much easier and less guilt-laden to believe something happened "suddenly!" rather than to think we have been lax in our attentiveness, and OH! how we are creatures of self-justification!

The truth is, I cannot honestly remember the last time I actually rode a bicycle. I haven't owned a motorcycle for thirty years, which weren't, in actuality, thirty "sudden" years but years that passed nanosecond by nanosecond. *Whoops!* Even so, why would I think I couldn't still ride one? As with many things in life, perhaps the "use it or lose it" theory *does* apply. I do know our math skills get rusty when we don't engage our brains in numbers; at least mine do. And our voices are throaty when we don't speak for long periods of time. We all recognize that craggy tone that proves we *did* awaken someone with our early-morning phone call, no matter how much they assure us we didn't. Our muscles become weak when we don't exercise them. Our teeth fall out when we forget to care for them . . .

But a lean? Who would imagine *that* could vanish? Could extra midlife pounds have thrown me off like that? But I've gained them equally on upper arms, thighs, the width of my feet . . . It's not like I packed all those pounds onto my right side, so how could *that* be it?

As I continue to compare "life's leans" to those needed on a moped or any other two-wheeled vehicle, I am aware that *life* happens best when we simply remember to freely ride it often enough to keep our balance rather than always trying to stiffen up, control it, and rein it in. Joy springs forth when we lean—as if relaxing into a soft pile of pillows—into the goodness and surprises that surround us rather than complaining about our perceptions of upcoming events before we've even lived a moment of them. We start wobbling when we find ourselves wasting the precious *now* by complaining about way back then—or even just a moment ago. I mean, what if I'd resurrected my old Flash Gordon can-do attitude and simply *played* at riding the moped rather than trying to conquer it? I bet there was a sparkly rock or shell along the roadside I could have picked up and used as my moped launcher. Goodness knows, I spent enough time roadside to find one.

Sometimes when we feel ourselves beginning to wobble, we just need to lighten up to regain our balance. After taking a moment here to quickly peruse my MP (you do the same), I can't think of a single time in my life when a positive attitude adjustment did not help, or would not have helped, me. What about you? A little whining never hurts anyone, but when we get stuck there . . . well . . .

Let me just toss in a *truly* "stuck there" story so you can see for yourself what choosing to stay stuck looks like. It's a *killer* of an embarrassing, unflattering story to tell about myself. (So you think I've already covered that ground? Well, you ain't heard nothin' yet!) I especially want you to ride your wobbling moped side by side with me here, exploring, *examining* times in your life when you might have allowed yourself to pull the same kind of thing. Perhaps you're hamstringing both yourself and your friends right now, so listen up!

❖❀❖

When I was working on my second book, *How to Eat Humble Pie & Not Get Indigestion*[1] (and wait until you hear how appropriately that title marries my mayhem!), our dear friends Al and Barb let me hide in their summer home. It was winter, I was writing (alone) in Al and Barb's house when I became ill. Really sick. Fever, trembling, aching, hacking-up-a-lung sick. Sick enough I needed to find a doctor's office, which isn't a pleasant thing to have to do when you're out of your territory. Bronchitis, sinus infection, drugs. Hack-hack. Blow nose. Poor me. Shiver, ache. Hack-hack. Repeat cycle for days on end, which turned into a couple weeks on end. All the while, type-type-type, since my deadline loomed. No rest for the wickedly sick running-behinders.

During the course of this terrible time, I phoned and e-mailed several friends. I am sick, said I. Please pray for my health and that I can stay focused and coherent enough to write words worthy of the topic since I am on whoop-de-doing drugs. Please pray for my sleep, which is missing. (Hack-cough, blow nose.) And so they did. After a couple weeks, home I came, still writing, still coughing. It was difficult to conduct a conversation since talking erupted into coughing. And laughing, fogeddaboudit! To laugh was to nearly end up choking to death. What a drag; what a painola to listen to! Two more rounds of drugs.

Then one day a friend called to check in on me again; she was one of many kind folks doing so on a regular basis. Although I was at long last on the road to recovery, when she asked me how I was, *I mustered up a cough*. Not that I never coughed anymore and not that my cough didn't still sound terrible when I did; but this time I *made* a cough happen, which then led to a bout of earnest coughing. "Better," I finally said, "but certainly not well." She'd keep praying, she said. Good.

After I hung up I said to myself, *What the heck was that, Charlene?!* I felt convicted enough (thank you, God!) to spend time assessing my motivation for such a despicable sham. Who in their right mind would wish themselves sicker than the reality?

Then it finally struck me: was I afraid that once I got well, my friends would no longer care about me as much? Apparently receiving all that attention and prayer had become habit-forming—and not in a good way. Through my own choice—my own *choice*—I was holding not only myself but my *friends* captive to my wobbly ego. Did I not know how much they would *rejoice* knowing that I, their friend, was once again back up to speed and that we could give *thanks* together and move on? Do lunch to celebrate?

❉ ❉ ❉

I am about to challenge you with a tough question, so buck up: Is it possible you are clinging to something negative from your past—something that was long ago over? Might you, to your own detriment, still be "living it" because you get so much attention for "it"? For repeating that story and tweaking it back to life with every new person you meet or as a reminder to those who've stood beside you but who occasionally sound weary of holding your wobbling self up, seeing you through?

Have your friends stopped calling, thereby hurling you into a pity party, when what is *really* pitiful is your own complaining self? Are you just used to thriving on crisis mode, even when the crisis passed months, maybe even years ago? (I can't *believe* I couldn't ride that moped!)

If this awakening smacks you like it did me (stop coughing!), it's time to conduct your own intervention, even if your friends haven't abandoned you. Make yourself take a cold, hard look at the possibility that *you* have given up, turned over—abandoned—your quest to live life to the full by putting a self-induced lid on it. Not that your incident wasn't terrible, but come on: is it time to just make up your mind to *be over it* and get happy again?

If you need to seek professional help to do this, get it. But sometimes we do not need to repeat the story again; we just need to let it go—tuck it away in the *archives* of our MPs, the ones we barely ever page back through.

Before moving on, stop here and pray. Think. Listen. *Be honest.*

❊ ❊ ❊

When we forget how to relax and naturally lean into the curves life tosses our way, when we forget how to see and seize life's goodness rather than putting our heads down in order to buck and shuck it off our backs like maniacal broncos (too quick with the gas; too quick with the brake; too quick with forecasting judgments, like "it's too hot for anything good"), we certainly cannot expect to *enjoy* our lives. When we choose to continue wallowing in an illness or incident that should no longer hold us back from rejoicing in what *is* good about our lives, we're back to hogtieing ourselves.

These concepts are neither rocket science nor new thoughts. But if we could just remember to live what we already know, we'd be brilliant at the game of life.

❊ ❊ ❊

Bret left the island the day before I did. Although I was going to keep my moped until the end, and although I was getting ever so slightly better by the time I turned it in, I didn't trust myself to be riding without him. Most times, the buddy system we learned in kindergarten is still the most sensible way to go through life. But neither did I come right home and borrow someone's bicycle to see how *that* might go for me. [MOMENT OF TRUTH: Still haven't. *Scare-dy cat!*]

Right this typing moment I have a choice: I can continue to spend more time bemoaning the fact that I've temporarily (*please!*) lost my moped-riding lean, or I can concentrate on the good memories from that event. Look, Charlene, in your own MP and sift through memories! See how they come into focus . . . the sound of my son's music, a potent private spiritual moment shared with the woman who booked me to speak on the island, the variations of blue in the ocean, sighting a barracuda while snorkeling, an exotic yellow bloom stubbornly growing up between the cement cracks, the spouse who frees me to gallivant from here to there to speak my passions and see all of this wonder, a prayer partner who prays for my trips . . . I pray that I may *never* forget these things, for their sum total is pure grace and gold.

Or I can miss another "five blocks" of now by further grumbling about two miles of wobbling back "then." It's my choice. It's your choice, too. What do you make of your past, lift up for your future, give to the now? What, in your choices and your MP, might help you notice, then recapture your natural lean?

7 * Splat
When We Crash and Burn Out

Several years after I started speaking on the topic of *Don't Miss Your Life!*, I began to wonder why I wasn't writing the book. (Okay, I had that crabby-body-part thing going, but that wasn't keeping my fingers from working since I wrote several other books throughout "those" days.) I certainly hadn't lost enthusiasm for the message; in fact, I grew more passionate about it. But life went on. I went on, and on, and on. No wobbling Weebling for me; I was all Energizer Bunny. Other book ideas surfaced and demanded my attention, and so I wrote them. But when I'd get done I'd always think, *Why aren't you writing* Don't Miss Your Life!?

"DMYL" became the identifying shorthand note I wrote on top of articles I snipped from newspapers and magazines, next to circled book paragraphs, on paper napkins, etc. I created a DMYL file for related bookmarked Web sites and relentlessly scribbled sentences flagged with *DMYL* in one of the notebooks I always keep tucked in my purse. My stacks of resources grew until I had to begin tossing the physical specimens into a plastic laundry basket to contain them. I collected e-mails in a DMYL file whose topical discussions and reminders screamed to be included in the one-day-to-be-written book. I continued traveling from here to there to present the message, and the basket (*all* resource forms) grew ever fuller. And yet I always tripped the trigger on a different project. The DMYL folder grew so big in physical contents and in my mind (feel me starting to bend under its weight?) that I undoubtedly needed a *major* pocket of time to even figure out where to begin. Familiar? But that giant pocket never seemed to arrive, just teensy zipper compartments of time in which I continued to gather yet more notes I later dumped in the DMYL mother-lode bin. I kept my globe-trotting self on the lookout for *more* thoughts, continued speaking my passions and feeding the DMYL monster as I could. After all, I was the queen of the DMYL message, the keeper of the codes, the fanner of everyone else's life-living flames.

Then one day, the unthinkable—the impossible—happened, the thing that *I* taught folks to watch out for (*Don't Miss Your Life!*), the thing that I felt above because I was so *wise* (feel the windup?): I burned out. Severely. I'd kept on and kept on until I'd moved *way* past losing my lean. As a result, I completely crash-landed.

You'd think that after I had that brilliant lost-my-lean awakening—not to mention nabbing that su-weet metaphor—I would have recognized the caution flags. In hindsight, I know I *did*! But to my own detriment, *I ignored them*. After all, I was the expert! (*Look* how much good stuff I've already told you right here in this book, how smart I am, how much I'm helping you!) I hope you can now understand the importance of that last chapter: I wrote it for *you*, from the shoes of the I-thought-I-was-above-that voice of experience. I do not want *you* to end up doing as I did but to do as I know *better* than to do: *keep* doing when what you need to do is to *stop*.

If you are feeling vulnerable to the big splat, I encourage you to flip right back to that last chapter and read it again, then take action. Relax. Play. Solicit your friends to help you—to help one another. Gather a few of your own magical touchstones and use them to launch yourself into something that refreshes you. Maybe it's staring at the sky; maybe it's a good game of tennis. Whatever, do it. Only arrogance tricks a person into thinking that the world—or a company, church, committee, family, or cause—can't go on without them while they take a time-out to refresh.

Read that last sentence again.

✳❇✳

After I crashed, the only prayer I could utter was *Help*, and sometimes that was too much to achieve. I couldn't even read a mindless novel; the words seemed to just drop off the page rather than string together. I could only wrap up in a blanket and stare into space. I didn't answer my phone. I didn't call my friends. It's like my hard drive was full. I simply could not add another kilobyte of information or process another request. My brain and body regressed into the spitting image of that terrible hourglass timer that appears when your computer has moved beyond thinking and seized up.

Oh, if only my recovery could have been as simple as a reboot! However, what I needed was a complete rebuild and revival, which would not, *could* not, come until after a long period of rest.

I've been asked how I worked my way out of this predicament. What did I do to shore myself up? How did I feel? When did I know I was getting better? I always hear the deeper question and, more important, recognize the desperate defeated voice of someone who's been there—or feels him- or herself on the edge. Someone who wants to know how they can more quickly get out of their pit the next time they splat. And yet my honest answer isn't one that *anyone* wants to hear, but here it is: I was helpless. I could do nothing. Nothing. I had no idea I was getting better. In fact, for about a week, I wasn't. I was floating in dark and un-familiar waters without a shoreline in sight. The only thing I had with me was my memory portfolio, and every recent entry was a blur—because that is what I'd been. What I clung to by a single weak thread was the *hope* that I could get better, but to be honest, I had no idea how long it would take or how I could go about help-ing myself. It's perhaps good news that I couldn't, since it kept me from striving to do *anything*. I simply rested, which is exactly what I needed to do. Light started returning only after my body and brain were rested enough that I could remember sweet MP entries from my precrash days. It's like I ripped out those pages and pasted them to my eyeballs so I could "see"—remember—why it was I *wanted* to be well.

In hindsight, of course I should have known better than to let things get to "that place." But when you have never been to "that place," you don't see it coming because you don't yet recognize it. Losing my metaphorical lean turned out to be the Big Red Flag, *a warning I did not heed*.

So was it lack of foresight that actually triggered my fall, that might trigger (or perhaps already has) yours?

I incrementally started setting the stage for my dramatic crash-and-burn nearly two years before it actually took place, when I began booking a few speaking engagements a couple years in my future—before I knew two book deadlines and three book tours in a year and a half would spring to life and land in the midst of them. Who among us can know what the future holds?

Many would look at my full-blown doomsville schedule and think, *What a wimp! This is what took you out? I've been living with that kind of schedule for years; it's just my norm. I thrive on that kind of ongoing adrenaline rush. Multitasking is my game!* And I would respond, if that is your norm, your natural-bent, true-self norm, good for you. But as for me and my sanity, not so. This I know to be true: we are different, you and me, and you and him, and him and her, and him and him, and each of God's children.

But is that your norm, your *healthy* norm? You better stop right now and honestly think about it lest you, too, splat.

❋ ❋ ❋

As opposed to popular opinion ("Surveys say . . ."), women are *not* all good multitaskers; all men are not mechanically inclined, and in order not to be sexist, vice versa. I'm pretty good with a wrench, but just give me one project at a time, please. While speaking in front of an audience of five thousand might melt the average Jason or Johanna, I can do it without a problem. Oh, sure, I get nervous before I go onstage. But once I'm out there and have uttered a few sentences, I'm so excited to be telling my stories that the time just flies. I believe when we use our natural gifts, great things happen with less effort. However, don't ask me to stay up late afterward to visit with you or to wait in a long line for dinner, because I won't be fun. Since I'm fed as an introvert (alone time, which shocks many people since I'm usually so lively in groups), I'll be drained empty after giving so much of myself. My "intake valve" (solitude and quiet, which includes writing) and "outflow passages" (speaking and traveling) need to remain balanced. If not, when I go to the well of energy,

I find it empty. When I am overtired, I am snarky beyond all reason. I am short-tempered, impatient, and can even be (seriously) flat-out rude.

I run out of nice.

When I am tired, empty, and out of nice, even though my mind is saying, *Patience, Charlene. Just be quiet,* and even after all these decades of *knowing* this about myself and fighting against it, my mouth still has a life of its own. No matter how much I pray about this, strive for change and accountability, and practice smiling through gritted teeth, the best thing I can do for myself and everyone around me is to ground me. I need to send me to my room, where I should stay until I can come out and play nice, which is usually after a quiet meal and a good night's sleep—unless the stream of more out than in goes on for weeks or months, which hurtles me into a whole new league of need.

Fasten your seat belt now as we step into my memory portfolio and "roll tape!" You'll see what I mean.

❉ ❉ ❉

During one three-day conference with several thousand attendees, I am one of many speakers both keynoting a session and presenting workshops. Two days in, I feel my batteries begging for a silent recharge. But alas, I have one more workshop to go. Since the event is not taking place in a hotel, where I can run to my room, I search the college until I find the girls' locker room in the gym. Dressed to the nines [MOMENT OF TRUTH: I was dressed to the six-and-a-halves], I nonetheless enter a shower stall and pull the curtain. I stand there (no water), leaning my head on the wall next to the soap dish and release a short, silent cry. Then I sit on the small wooden bench and pray until the last possible minute before I have to hike to the next session. *Lord, if it's you who lives within and not me, then you better start talking because I'm flat out of nice words!* As I walk onto the stage, an inexplicable (yea, God!) gust of energy sweeps into my body and stays with me until I am done—at which point I again deflate.

It is no longer I who live,

but Christ lives in me.

GALATIANS 2:20

At the very end of the conference, while I'm packing up my book table and hoping nobody will talk to me (nice, eh?), I take note of a sister speaker prowling the halls for just one more person to have an exchange with. *How does she do it?* Then I realize (enlightenment!) that God created her to be energized by people, while I, on the other hand, am drained by people—even though I love the exchanges with them. A *good* drain, but nonetheless a drain. *I wonder if the solitude of writing is hard on her?*

I've gone on to learn it is.

❊ ❊ ❊

I cannot judge myself or my ability by comparing my actions to others' since God made us each different—some of us (ahem) more "different" than others. Neither can you. 'Tis good to know your limits by knowing and honoring them, not by comparing them to someone else's.

✻✿✻

But it is during yet another huge conference that I learn the value and *necessity* of grounding myself. [MOMENT OF TRUTH: I learn almost everything the hard way.] This time, even though my room is attached to the convention center via a maze of hallways and elevators, there isn't time between sessions to get there and back. I can't find anything close to a quiet locker-room haven, so I just keep hanging on and hanging on until the last session is over. I am on the edge. I finally get into an elevator alone (*Whew!*) and am just about to release a deep breath when one of the conference workers sticks her hand between the closing doors and holds on until they bounce open so she can enter.

"I am so glad I ran into you!" (See her poke my arm to make her point as she speaks.) She explains that a group of the volunteers is going to gather at the pool to party. I am just (another poke) who they need to cheer them up since I am "so funny."

The elevator begins to stop at every floor, more people crowding in, moving us closer together. I feel a bout of *really* not nice rising up inside me. I scoot a few inches to my left, hopefully out of her poking reach while I thank her for her invite and explain that I'm sure they'll get along fine without me.

"But you *gotta*"—(major poke)—"come!"

"Seriously," say I, my molars starting to grind, "I'm really crabby and tired right now. It's best I go to my room."

"Oh, come *on!*" she exclaims while delivering a light smack to my arm. "How crabby could *you* possibly *ever* be?!" After all, I'm the lively and funny one, remember? People often say, "I wish you were my neighbor!" To which I respond, "Talk to my neighbors." Right, Burl, Ginger? How crabby could I ever be? she wants to know.

[MOMENT OF TRUTH: Here's exactly how I answer.] "So

crabby that I'm thinking if you poke me one more time, I might deck you." There is not a hint of "so funny" in my voice. I cannot tell you emphatically enough how much I *mean* it.

Here is the thing about being a known humorist: as she doubles over laughing, she pokes me again. "You are too funny! What a HOOT! *HAHAHAHAHAHA!*"

Luckily for both of us, the elevator door opens and she hops off with a "see you at the pool!" over her shoulder. She's still laughing as the door closes. I, on the other hand, feel my eyes start to sting. Thankfully I make it to my room without another human encounter. I close the door, tear off my evil panty hose, sprawl across my bed, and cry over the utter *wretch* that I am! Utter. Wretch.

And yet, God blessed my presentations since I later heard about them, many times over. In spite of my wretchedness, God blessed and used my nice words and cloaked my cruel ones, neither of which I deserved.

Utter wretch.

Grace.

I once heard a woman pray that if we at that particular retreat uttered cruel or misplaced words, God would cause a crop failure on them so they didn't take root. I have prayed that prayer many times since. Do I use it as an excuse to allow for my occasional meltdowns? May it never be! But when my feet of clay win out (because I do the very things I do not want to do), I pray 'em with fervor.

Before my splatting burnout—which I will herewith bravely call a breakdown since I have yet to figure out the languaging difference between them—even though I was tired, I had to just keep trudging on. [MOMENT OF TRUTH: Did I? I've asked myself many times since. The world would have gone on without me. Sure, some people would have been disappointed, but I wouldn't have abused myself by rendering myself no earthly good to anyone for a long while.] I spoke, I emoted, I gave of myself, told my stories, got on one airplane after another during my book tours, signed books, spoke here, traveled there, gave another weekend retreat, and then—and *then*—I drove on another eight-hundred-mile book-signing road trip that I engineered (as opposed to the one my publisher set up) because I studied only the dots on my calendar rather than also considering the pre-dot preparation time, personal energy drains during the dots, and lack of "in" refueling time between those dots. (I encourage you to reread the portion of that sentence starting with ". . . because I . . .") I remember driving along crying when my cell phone rang. It was my agent wanting to know how I was holding up. I tried to hide my nasally, giveaway weeping voice, but I felt myself starting to lose the battle. I pulled into a restaurant parking lot and just sobbed. (Red flags: whining *and* crying.) And still, there were two more events to go.

"Charlene, you need to stop," she said. But I couldn't. (Right?) Appointments were on my calendar, people were expecting me. I was *so important*.

I was so important that I didn't take care of me. (Relatable?) *What's wrong with that picture?!*

A quick two-night unpack at home, wash clothes, pack back up, answer e-mails and go through snail mail, then *another* 298-mile drive to the last book presentation and book signing, the one I barely made it through—although I remember weeping a couple times, thank goodness during stories that had a tenderness element to them. The audience had no idea there was more to it than met the eye, although I did tell them "this" (snort, snot, wipe tears) sometimes happened to me when I was tired. By the time I drove up the six-mile hill to this respite where I come to write (hereafter called The Farm), I could barely see to drive. I'm not sure what might have happened to me if I hadn't had this rented old farmhouse of my heart (at that time, we'd been renting it for about a year, and thankfully that last book stop was here in the area) to come to that night. It's possible I'd have ended up in a motel room or maybe even a hospital or psych ward. Seriously. I can't be sure. I spoke to nobody but my husband, whom I called and told I'd fallen apart. Did I want him to come? No. I didn't want to see anyone, not a single soul. After a week of nothing-ness, I could finally take baby steps, but each one exhausted me. Slowly, I noticed I could move without crying or collapsing. All in all, it took nearly two months before my energy returned to anything resembling normal and three months before I truly felt myself again.

When I crack open my MP to those wounded days, I remember picking up my Bible and thinking how foreign the familiar words looked. *Help*. I remember turning on the television and having no clue what the people were saying. I remember waking up, surprised I'd napped yet again. I remember not showering or getting dressed for days, leaving the curtains closed, and eating whatever was in the fridge and cabinets because I couldn't muster a trip to the grocery store.

My husband would call and tell me this friend or that wanted to know how I was doing. "Do not have them call me!" Are you okay? he asked. "No." Did I want him to come *now*? "No." When did I think I'd be coming home? "I have no idea. I hope soon. But I can't come home until I can at least drive without crying, until I can breathe without effort." Did I need anything? "Yes, pray for me since I can't even pray for myself." And so he did. And so God held me, rocked me, and, I realize now, by grace helped me to *stay down* and lean on him, which is just where I needed to be leaning.

✻ ✱ ✻

But even out of the ashes rises redemption. The answer to *why* I wasn't writing DMYL so very long ago is now so obvious: had I not experienced a serious burnout before writing this book, I could not offer *you* the gift of "Yes, I *do* know what it feels like to be so fried that you are incapable of helping yourself. I *do* know what it feels like to completely fall apart. I *can* now speak with authority about being rendered useless by my own arrogant and ego-driven determination to continue doing that which I could not."

If you feel *yourself* falling and are no longer *able* to allow yourself to lean into life—in other words, you feel like you're about to crack in half from the pace and pressure—lean on *my* experience and learn from it. It's important that you do it now, before it's too late.

Do you believe God and no other humans on Earth are capable of helping orchestrate a backup plan during your respite, say like babysitting or taking over that project? Has it occurred to you that maybe the backup plan *is* God's perfect and better plan for a time—for *everyone*, no matter how tangentially involved?

Put that in your pondering pipe and puff on it for a while.

8 ✻ i'm sick of listening to me

Bye-Bye, Old Tapes and Negative Thinking

I occasionally have strong opinions and I'm not afraid to share them, even when common sense tells me I shouldn't. Not only that, but I think I interrupt people too often. Not always on purpose; sometimes words just blurt out before I've had a chance to clamp my mouth shut. And not that some people don't need to pipe down (say, someone elbowing me in an elevator) but it's not always my job to help them do so. Plus, no matter how many times I tell myself that tomorrow (notice that is not today, which is proof that procrastination is yet *another* of my pitfalls) I will work even harder to change this or that about my behaviors, far too often the intention doesn't last longer than the thought. Like how every day I say I'm going to start walking more, which Kornflake, our big red mutt dog, would truly appreciate should I decide to take him along—even when he *doesn't* have to pee.

Plus, I fret about things, like if I had quit chewing my finger-nails a couple decades ago, might I still have my gallbladder? Al-though I'm not exactly sure what my gallbladder did for its life's work, I can't imagine sharp, gnarly pieces of fingernail did it any good.

And what if I wasn't so quick-tempered sometimes? What if I hadn't crashed and burned? What if I hadn't lost that race, or been late with my report, or snarked at George—again? And if I'd get better at "all things in moderation," I wouldn't have to spend so much time chastising myself for eating too many Cheetos—or eating too much of anything.

(Take a breath here, then expel a long deep exhale . . .)

And you might not believe this, but I'm terrible when it comes to . . .

* ✿ *

Does this type of onslaught of negative, self-belittling think-ing sound familiar to you? If so, no wonder you're missing your life! It's not that I get stuck in this kind of loop very often. But on occasion, say, after I've interrupted someone or held the Cheetos bag over my open mouth so the last remaining particles of Cheeto dust don't go to waste, the negative diatribing begins.

SOMEBODY SMACK ME! Especially since everyone knows that emotional eaters need a snack when they're feeling poorly about themselves!

But of uppermost importance, this type of negative tape, which could be sold as your Value Package since it covers so many topics in one long breath, is an affront to the honor of every God-given breath we draw. It also makes for a boring, predictable, miser-able life.

Boredom: a constantly revolving roadblock in our path to joy.

Oh, the negative tapes we relentlessly play in our heads, some of them instilled in us by our parents, others by schoolyard taunters, coworkers, strangers at stoplights . . . Oh, the miles of hurtful words we can lay down to ourselves at the end of the day (or worse yet, the beginning), so many that we could build a sidewalk straight to insanity with them. "If I've told you once, I've told you a thousand times . . ." And so we have. We've told ourselves the same exhausting and depressing things over and over until we are just certain about them.

Not that we shouldn't aspire to personal growth and improvement; but to build our foundation on negative soil is dumb. Not that I haven't been dumb before, or wasted huge pockets of time obsessing over which earrings to wear, or driven five brainless blocks, or accidentally sent an inflammatory e-mail to the wrong e-mail address, or belched in the middle of a speech or lost my lean or . . .

STOP!

If it isn't clear by now, negative thinking breeds more negative thinking. Negative thinking about ourselves usually results in harsher judgments about others, which causes us to feel even worse about ourselves for judging them, and I hate when I do that!

STOP! STOP! STOP!

One Sunday Pastor Christine uttered a perfectly misspoken word. She meant to say "sarcasm," but instead it out came "scarcasm." *Ouch!* I wrote that down on the front of my bulletin, never to be forgotten, because isn't that the truth?! All acerbic, sarcastic, negative words hold the power to scar a person, and we don't want to be the ones logging them in anyone's MP, including our own.

If your life feels all doom and gloom, maybe it's because the needle of your thoughts has slipped into a pessimistic and sarcastic groove. Time to change the record and start playing some new tunes for yourself and those around you, which is exactly what I'm here to help you do. Let us begin with Kornflake, who just gave me another good and timely example of the evils (and dumbness) of negative thinking and self–trash talk, even though his momentary behavior was that of a very bad boy. Although I'm sure he didn't think of his behavior as bad. No, I'd say from the looks of his airborne tongue, he thought his runaway romp was fun! Perhaps the most fun he's had since we adopted him.

Since I'm currently up here at The Farm (thankfully not splatted!), I'm in an area that offers lots of enticing doggie distractions, like cats, cows, horses, squirrels, toads, and scents galore. It's not that our suburban home in Illinois doesn't offer distractions, too, but kids, other dogs, and George just aren't as fascinating. (Nothing personal, dear.) So I was at The Farm, out playing ball with Kornflake when he delivered his "fine example." He was off leash, which I allow only when we're fully engaged. Today I was using my wrist rocket to launch tennis balls, which he chases and returns to my feet, then ecstatically, excitedly, waits for me to launch the next one. RIGHTNOWRIGHT-NOWRIGHTNOW! However, rather than dropping the ball at my feet, he galloped right by me. I turned my head to witness him slinking under the electric fence, straight toward the very surprised band of cows that had quietly snuck up the hill to about twelve feet behind me when I wasn't looking. Kornflake had seen them hundreds of times before, say, when he'd been on his leash or tied out on the porch, but he'd never paid much attention to them—or so I thought. Apparently he was just waiting for the moment they were up here with us and he was off leash to engage in the lively art of the chase.

Typically, they appear over the ridge of the hill, like a puppet appears from below the stage: I first see their ears and exotic spiky hairdos, then their heads. Lumber, lumber, and there they are. But this time because I had my back to the field, I didn't even know they were up the hill until away they all disappeared back down over the ridge of the hill, a black-and-white thundering blur of stampeding cows—a big red dog hot on their trail. Out of sight they went, all of them. I ran to the fence and couldn't remember which of the three wires was "live," plus I doubted I'd fit between any of the openings without electrocuting myself, so I stood there and screamed, "KORNFLAKE! KORNFLAKE! COME!"

Since I could no longer see them, imagined disaster played in my head as I continued to scream. A serious bout of dwelling on the negative overcame me. *Kornflake would get kicked in the head and die.* Or he'd corral the herd down there and tackle a sweet calf, thinking it wanted to play with him. Or they'd all be running downhill so fast they'd go *through* a fence at the other end of the pasture—which I can't see and don't even really know exists— and the farmer would have me jailed, my dog shot, or vice versa. Or Kornflake would keep on running *past* the cows, through the fence, and out into the wilderness, where he'd be discovered weeks later, bone skinny, covered with mud, and smelling bad—just like he was by the gentleman who turned him in to the humane society whence we got him. While imagining all of this (dwell, dwell, dwelling on the disastrous!), I continued screaming. "KORNFLAKE! KORNFLAKE! COME!"

Then, appearing up over the top of the ridge, I saw first the crown of Kornflake's bobbing head, then his flopping ears, then his airborne flapping tongue. He was flying straight toward me, obviously exhilarated by his brief journey. He was ready to chase the next ball. I wanted to tackle him, throttle him, tell him, "BAD BOY! YOU NEARLY GAVE MOMMY A HEART ATTACK!" But I knew that would be the worst thing I could do, since he would think I'd punished him for *returning*. So I reinforced the positive. (Nearly all dog-training books agree with this.) "Good boy! You came home." Zing went the ball, off he went after it. But then . . . here came the cows up over the hill—again! Either they'd enjoyed the chase or they are a group of self-loathing cows who "negative-talked" themselves into coming back for more. Or they're just dumb. Or were curious enough to see if it would happen again, which is where I'd put my money since they are the nosiest things on Earth. To say I tackled my dog would not be an overstatement; I must have looked like I was auditioning for the NFL! Still, I did not yell. Once I got myself up off the ground, maintaining my grip on his collar, I stayed calm, petted his silky ears, brought him in, and gave him a treat. In the future, I will look into training methods to deal with this issue, but until then, when the cows are around, Kornflake will not be off leash.

❖ ✿ ❖

I hope you noticed *your* applicable lesson in that story. In case you missed it, let me spell it out for you: Give yourself positive reinforcement for what you do right, even if and when you don't get *all* of it right. Dwell on your positive attributes (sure, I fell down, but I got *up* again, which means I'm persistent!) and vow to continue allowing God to work on the shortcomings. Would Kornflake ever want to come back to me if I beat him up for it?

Why would I want to continue living in my own skin if my every waking thought is one that beats me up?

Why would you?

❖ ✿ ❖

Even Willie Nelson says in *The Tao of Willie*,[1] "Once you replace negative thoughts with positive ones, you'll start having positive results." Willie. Now, there's a guy who spent far too long in Nashville trying to change who he was to satisfy the advice of others. Not until he decided to *be* who he was (pigtails and all) did he emerge as the Willie whose music comprises many of the notes in my veins. (Nobody sings "Stardust" better than Willie!) Is he perfect? Certainly not. But the fruits of his attitude and perseverance have blessed me. If you can't believe God, Willie, and *The Little Engine That Could*, perhaps it's time you listened harder. Especially to God. And if you *still* can't believe in your ability to overcome negative thinking, believe in God's ability to do it for you.

❖ ❖ ❖

While writing the *Welcome to Partonville* series, when I was truly out of my own way, *remarkable* things happened. But before I could fly in my labors, I had to step around the temptation to talk myself out of it. I had to quit reciting the multiple negative reasons why I wasn't talented enough to be writing fiction—that is, no education to do so, small vocabulary, no college degree in anything, don't read enough literary publications, don't know half the verbs academia uses . . . Once I open the door to self-doubt, the list goes on and on. But set aside, oh, *baby*, what *fun*! When you hear authors say the story (which I'm convinced always knows more than the authors do) runs like a movie in their heads, believe them; it's true. But the movie has no space to run if the mind is already full of gloomy "can't do! not worthy!" trailers.

Case in point. During a phone chat with a group of book-club members who'd read the series, one of the ladies asked me how I ever came up with the marvelous idea to have Dorothy, my eighty-seven-year-old heroine, talk to her smile. She told me she's since applied the advice from the fictional scene to her real life, and that it works wonders.

"It just 'happened,'" I said in all honesty.

When another participant asked about the source of that particular scene, I had to explain that no, my mother never talked to *me* about talking to my smile in order to coax it out on a gloomy day, as the fictional Dorothy's mother talked to her in my story. However, my mother did smile most of the time. Smiled, hummed, sang, and kept a positive spirit. I went on to explain that once I was out of my own way—in other words, after I lifted the anchor on my own defeat—I believe the memory of my mother's smile "called forth" the following pared-down excerpt from *Dearest Dorothy, Help! I've Lost Myself!*

The flashback setting (for Dorothy, too—even my fictional characters use their MPs!) is this: Dorothy, a stubborn nine-year-old girl at the time, does not want to change into her Sunday clothes for church. The clock is ticking down the time. After several volleys of verbal standoff, Ethel, Dorothy's exasperated mother, takes her into the bathroom, where they both stand facing the mirror, daughter in front of mother.

"Dorothy Jean Brown, we both look pathetic. Just get a good gander at us. I think we should talk to our smiles and try to coax them out of their hiding places. After all, if you were the Pastor, would *you* want to look at these faces while you were preaching God's word?"

Mother and daughter spent a few moments moving nothing but their eyes between their reflections. Pretty soon, it became impossible not to giggle, which is exactly what they did.

"Look at us," Ethel said. "Don't we look like *fine* women when we smile?"

"We *do*," Dorothy said, her heart erupting with love for her mother like an explosion of happy feathers.

"Let us determine right here and now," Ethel said, resting her hands on her daughter's shoulders, "that when we find we haven't been smiling enough, we will talk to our smiles to encourage them, okay? We'll talk to our smiles until we *feel* them rumbling around inside of us. We'll talk to our smiles until they appear, so that when we look in the mirror, we can smile back at them." Ethel then leaned over and kissed the top of her daughter's fine brown hair, her warm breath melting Dorothy's remaining resistance.

Without another word, Dorothy Jean Brown quickly changed into her blue dress, casting a hurried eye into her dresser mirror each time she passed it, just to make sure she was smiling back at . . . her smile.

And now, nearly eight decades later, Dorothy Jean Wetstra talked to her smile yet again, realizing it had been hiding for several days. . . .

[She] stretched her 5'10" frame and walked down the hall to her bathroom, reaching her arm around the corner to flick on the light. . . .

"Come on, smile," she said out loud to her face in the mirror. "I know you're in there; I've seen you in many photos over all these decades. You know, it's band practice tonight and Nellie Ruth will be here within thirty minutes to pick us up. Do you want her or Raymond, the director, who stands *right* in front of us so I can hear him with these old ears, to have to look at *this* face while I'm trying to muster enough air to blow through my clarinet?" She put her hands to her hips, cocked her head, bugged out her eyes, and lifted her brows in a challenging gesture. "I mean think about all the friends and happy melodies we'll be surrounded by. Think about the goodness the Lord has blessed us with by allowing me the privilege to even *have* a face—although Lord, I sometimes do wonder *what* You are thinking when letting it age into *this*!" . . .

Yes, that outward appearance was constantly changing. But the thing that disturbed her most was the lack of any evidence of a grateful smile for all that blessed her. "Come on smile, I know you're in there!" *We'll talk to our smiles until we feel them rumbling around inside of us*, she heard her mother saying.

She closed her eyes, willing herself to examine what she *was* feeling. Sad? Lonesome? Lost? Old?

Then a subtle shift birthed in her gut. "Oh, my," she whispered, goose bumps racing up her arms. What she could *feel* was her mother's heavenly hands on her shoulders, her soft breath on the crown of her head. For a good fifteen seconds, she stood motionless, receiving this gift of grace. When she opened her eyes, nearly expecting to see her mother once again standing behind her, only her own reflection appeared in the mirror. But so did her smile.

"There now. That's better. What a *fine* woman you look like when you smile," she said, wiping the joyful tears of love and remembrance from the soft wrinkles around her welcome and familiar grin. "Thank you, Lord, for the balm of sweet memories. Let the winds of change blow where they will; as long as I remember You and my smile, I believe life will go as it should."[2]

I could not have written that scene, which just blessed me again as I read it, had I allowed my own negative thinking to block the gateway to the mysteries of creativity. (*You're not good enough, smart enough, educated enough . . . clever enough. Turn off your computer*.) Rather than trusting in myself, I turned off the negative faucet, which is often a snaky form of false humility anyway (worth a rewind of a read), and trusted the unearned, undeserved gift God has given me to collect and tell stories. I repeat: I trusted God and God's gift to me, not Charlene's talent or lack thereof.

Ask Yourself: What endeavor might you be conquering if you weren't instead wasting your energy on negative talk? How much lighter might you feel if you left the heavy weight of your own self-doubt behind? What gift has God given *you* that you've refused to trust?

❋ ❋ ❋

I am currently seated on a vintage chrome-and-red-vinyl kitchen chair I purchased a couple years ago for three dollars at a garage sale. I dragged it out on the front porch along with a small table, my laptop, a freshly brewed glass of iced tea, notes, my cell phone, a bouquet of dandelions I picked earlier, and Kornflake, who is secured to the house with a long rope—and you know why. It's seventy-eight degrees here at The Farm (I just went and looked). It's partly cloudy, but the sun is out more than it's hiding behind the racing clouds. My face and arms are pleasantly warm. I'm wearing jeans, a long-sleeved T-shirt with the sleeves pushed up to my elbows, and a brightly flowered baseball cap that's at least fifteen years old. Welcome to my world of glamour.

As you know, I've been writing about both my real-life mother and a scene where a character's mother talks to her young daughter about their smiles. And . . .

I am smiling.

Since I've been dwelling on what is good and right and true, I *feel* it enough that it shows on my face. When, many paragraphs earlier, I was beating myself up, I can guarantee you I was un-doubtedly scowling.

What *I* will take away from writing this chapter (thank you, God!) is proof that what I am saying here is true. We do find what we look for, and I want to find my own face smiling at all the goodness in my life, like my returning dog, the warmth of the sun on my arms, the funky cowlicky hairdos on the cows—and the memory of my mother's smile. I want to put and keep these things in my memory portfolio and hug it to my chest.

How about you stop here and take a moment to quickly (as in no dwelling) collect a few of your most tried-and-true (as in down the drain I go) negative tapes. Put them in an imaginary box and heave them into your garbage can. Throw away the BAD SELF, YOU RAN AWAY! kind of tapes so you can replace them with the GOOD SELF, YOU CAME BACK! kind.

Seriously, do this mental exercise. Toss out the junk.

Ahem. I'm waiting here while you do it . . .

God created human beings; he created them godlike, reflecting God's nature. He created them male and female. God blessed them: "Prosper! Reproduce! Fill Earth! Take charge!"

GENESIS 1:27 MSG

Look at all that space you have in there now! Think about the wonderful memories, the beautiful bright spots in your life that can fill it in and grow their own roots. Plus, now that you've quit trash-talking to yourself, you have time to listen for a new voice, a positive voice, a bigger voice, a God voice of approval. The Voice of a God who created you.

Yes, you are God's creation, just the way you are—even if you go garbage picking for a few of those negative tapes when you're done with this chapter. God is *always* glad when you return.

"Thank you for coming home, child of mine. Good child. GOOD child!"

9 * trust the question

And the Question Would Be?

One day a couple years ago, George was feeling under the weather. I told him to just rest and take it easy, but you know how we are. We just keep slugging along. Going to work. Breathing our germs all over everyone there so they, too, can get sick and not stay home. (Beware the lean; don't forget about the *splat.*) But since George is retired and, well, *is* home, he was busy spreading his germs throughout the house rather than just staying in bed. I heard him going up and down the stairs, in and out of doors, scrambling around doing anything other than letting his body rest, but I'd long ago given up trying to tell him what to do. [MOMENT OF TRUTH: I try to tell George what to do several times a day, but I was working under a deadline, so I decided to put my energy where it would actually do some good.]

There's something else you need to know about me because it factors into the story: I don't like to be interrupted when I'm writing, especially when I'm working on fiction, which I was doing on this particular day. (Unless you call me to do lunch, at which point I drop everything and go.) My home office is ten by ten and packed with furniture and overflowing piles. Although my desk faces a window, I don't like to keep the door closed because it gets too warm in there. But when I leave the door open, George, who passes by the door twenty-seven hundred times a day, always needs to ask me just one little question, thinking if the question is small enough, it won't interrupt the flow of words I've just spent the last *four hours* accumulating in my head and that are finally starting to pour forth. After hundreds of explanations as to why even a one-word question or statement is still an interruption (hear *me* sigh a billion times—then watch me go completely *ballistic*), George finally gets the clue: don't interrupt when I'm writing.

One day I heard his footsteps coming up the stairs (my office is at the top), but rather than passing on by to the room where his computer resides, those size-thirteen footsteps stopped outside my open office door. Where they remained. I tried to ignore this new tactic, then finally swiveled my chair and asked the man standing there staring at the back of my head, *"WHAT?!"*

"I didn't interrupt," he said, actually believing himself. "I was waiting until you stopped typing."

Sigh.

The next day I went shopping for a stick-on mirror, which I applied to the edge of my computer monitor. "See this, George? If I can see you in my rearview mirror, you are interrupting me." Even though the man is a saint for putting up with me, he can occasionally be an annoying and untimely saint. After all these decades, this is the way our marriage goes.

Now back to the day he wasn't feeling well, which is about two years into our reflection system. I hear the footsteps, then in my rearview mirror I see George park himself outside my office door, where he stands until I whirl like a maniacal dervish. *"WHAT?!"*

"Do you know where we keep the thermometer?"

He's sick. I want him to get well. I hate it when I feel guilty, which I now absolutely am because the man is *sick* and he's asking me about the thermometer. I take a deep breath and tell him that I don't think we ever replaced the one we broke some years earlier. *Thank you, Lord, for the wellness we've obviously enjoyed since then.* Then he asked the follow-up question I shall never forget. "You mean we don't even have one of our old baby thermometers around?"

I'm sure my eyebrows snapped so quickly up my forehead that they likely disappeared over the back of my head. Our "baby" was, at this point, around thirty-five years old, which means that when he was a baby, we weren't using ear thermometers that take your temperature—via your *ear*. Nor did we take baby's temperature in the mouth. I doubt I need to spell out exactly what pathway those oldies entered. I sat staring at him, my mouth agape.

"Does that mean no?" he asked, in all seriousness.

"I don't even want to *know* why you're asking me such a question, George."

He furrowed his eyebrows until I reminded him what you've already figured out, then he laughed. Thank goodness! "Guess we need a new one."

Righto.

Although this chapter is called "Trust the Question," I'm assuming the question you might, at any given time, be wrestling with is a sane one, like "Should I get married?" (Interesting that this is the first question that popped into my mind after telling the previous thermometer story.) Or "Why did I get married?"

(*Whoops!* Just kidding, George.) Or "What was he thinking?" (Okay, I'm letting this go now.) Or maybe your question is a potent and demanding one, like "Where is God?" Or, "*Is* God?" "How do I know if I should take this job?" "Is it true what she said about me?"

One of my biggest Life Questions surfaced right after my heart-stopping episode. "Why, God, was life pumped back into me and not into my mother? *Why?*"

When I first asked God this question, which occasionally still floats through my thoughts, I didn't exactly feel survivor's guilt, although I can at least now somewhat imagine what that must be like, say, to be the one in ten who survives a coal-mine cave-in or tragic airline crash. Who among us deserves to be that person? I've also never felt anger when I've asked God to explain this great mystery to me. I just feel the question, some-times with more intensity than others. But the more time that passes, the more I've learned to trust the question, since I real-ize it keeps me talking to God. It's as though God says, "That's for me to know and for you to find out via me, child of mine." But God doesn't say it with that *neener-neener*, thumb-in-ears-finger-wagging taunt of youth. No, God says it with the tone of voice that assures me that I will either one day know the answer, or that one day I will no longer have the question since the answer will simply no longer matter.

Sometimes when I'm praying, or staring into space at a cloud formation, or watching the Kentucky Derby (God's beautiful, powerful creatures in perfect motion, a sight that often makes me cry), or fishing, or telling a story about my mom or dad, like the tea-and-honey moment—all, in their own ways, forms of prayer—bubbles of God-knowledge, aglow with iridescent colors, float into my consciousness. They seem to hint at pieces of the answer. Like "You wouldn't understand the depth of the reverberation of your mother's hum if it didn't come to you all the way from heaven." Or "How could you reach the hearts of others who have lost loved ones if you had no knowledge of the depth of loss?" [MOMENT OF TRUTH: Or the curious bubble that reminds me that it wasn't until after my mother died—and because of her death—that I began to walk closely with God.] Then the bubble— the bright, fragile, blessed bubble of grace and mercy hinting at answers—floats off as quietly as it arrived, and I am once again left with the question. Gratefully, it doesn't feel quite as large or looming. Surely the breath of God blows these transcendent bubbles into our lives.

As I continue to ask God hard questions about death and loss, my own ever-growing MP shores up my belief that I am asking the right entity. I can't imagine what it would have been like *without* God. How would I have come through the grief of losing my mother and, decades later, my father, without clinging to the God who enfolds me under his gentle wing, catches my tears as if they were sacred pearls, quiets his lost sheep, soothes me, calls me unto himself in the Word, saying, *Let us therefore draw near with confidence to the throne of grace, that we may receive mercy and may find grace to help in time of need* (Hebrews 4:16 NASB). As you reread that sweet woo, notice that grace and mercy lead us to God, who has the answers.

God, who *is* the answer.

OH! A *brilliant* circling bubble of knowledge!

Poof.

And still, the questions come. *Am I qualified? Should I trust this thought?*

And we want answers, now.

Why can't I stop being impatient, God?

✱❋✱

Decades ago, my friend Mar and I started calling "Dibs!" when we'd see an older woman—*the* older woman—we wanted to be when *we* got old. Of course said perfect older woman would be perky, colorfully dressed, stylish (in her own funky way), and engaged with life, and would absolutely not wear the old-lady "round 'do," as we referred to it, upon her head. Nor would she be carrying a white vinyl handbag. These things, we determined, made an old woman a dead giveaway as an old woman. Perhaps the old male equal would be that of black socks, white tennis shoes, and plaid shorts.

If two old women were walking down the sidewalk and one exhibited our benchmark for the future, whoever saw them first would call, "I get to be the one on the right!" No arguments. A call was a call. This odd "game" (dare I say rude game—although we didn't mean it to be that way, in fact still don't, since we still play) spread to greeting cards. We started noticing, buying, and sending each other cards that had at least two women on them, the sender making note on the card as to which of the two *we*, the sender, were.

I've kept probably a dozen of those cards, and I'm looking at one now. Mar sent it to me for my birthday in 2000, the year I was old enough to take the "55 Alive" driving course from AARP. I made note of the year, then put it in my ever-growing DMYL laundry basket from which I'm plucking. The cover of the card is a hilarious vintage black-and-white photograph of nine women who are running down a gravel road. Each is wearing either a dress or a skirt and blouse, and all but one is wearing an apron. They are running side by side and appear to be engaged in a competition since each has a skillet in one hand, which they're using to flip pancakes high into the air. All the faces are laughing, mouths agape, eyes up or down, depending upon where their pancake is in this freeze-frame. You cannot help but at least smile when you look at this picture. Such abandon, joy, silliness, camaraderie. Along with the greeting on the inside, Mar has written, "I am #3 on the left."

I am #3 on the left. Such a bold, claiming statement.

Of course I flip back to the card's cover picture after reading the note and wonder why. Number three's pancake isn't the highest in the air; number four holds that honor. Number three isn't as busty as the real Mar (hmm) but she appears to be taller than my friend, which might have influenced Mar's call, since she's shorter than taller. Number three's head is tilted back the farthest. After a good study, I suspect it's because she's launched an errant flip that caused her pancake, which looks to be folding in half—perhaps it's on its way down—to be going backward over her head.

But not until after I've now studied the picture for a *very* long time do I notice that while the rest of the women are wearing clunky shoes with their hose (although number nine is wearing socks folded down at the ankles), number three is wearing cowboy boots!

Booger! *I* want to be number three! It's *my* birthday! (Well, it was back in 2000.) *I* should get to be number three! But alas, Mar called it, and so it must forever be. Which leaves me with this burning question: then which one am I?

Which of course leads me to *Who am I, really?*

This is not the first time I've asked *that* question. Who am I? WHO am I? Who AM I?

Who am I—a laughing, yelling, sensitive, and insensitive doofus all rolled into one complicated, frustrating, and glorious package—that God should love me? That God should not only

desire for me to live life to the full but to encourage everyone else
to do the same?

✻❋✻

Back in the early nineties, I went to a writer's workshop and
struck up a lively and rich friendship with one of the participants. We two stay-at-home moms shared much in common, including a desire to dink around writing a novel together, and so
we did. Although said novel didn't sell (one of these days, when
we have nothing *else* to do ... HA!), within a couple years I had
my first book contract, albeit nonfiction, and Mary Beth had a
child with cancer. Did I think I deserved this? Did I think Mary
Beth deserved this?

God? *GOD!*

In the midst of my unrelenting wrestling with these questions,
I took a trip to Oregon to visit another good friend, which only
heightened the anxiety of my questions, since Mary Beth sure
couldn't take a vacation; she was fighting for her daughter's life!
For two days of our visit we rented a condominium right on the
ocean. On the second afternoon I rolled up my pant legs, put on
my jacket to ward off the fall winds, and took a long stroll on the
beach alone. There were things I wanted to talk to God about.

I was very aware of the smallness of self against the crashing
vastness of God's ocean. The cool water swirled around my toes,
tickling them as the remnants of the waves backwashed out away
from me and pulled some of the sand from beneath my feet. Ever
so gently, grain by grain, the sand loosed and lowered me into
God's earth. It was so gentle; yet I knew that death hovered near
should I wade out and get caught in the undertow of one of the
huge breakers. Once, when I was a child, I was pulled under by
the sea's force. Tossed and turned and choking, my body was fi-

nally deposited on the shore by the grace of God. Yes, I know the ocean's power.

In the stretching shadows of the late of day, I finally gave in to my unrest and approached God's throne, the one God calls us to, which can be found anywhere we need God. Although, after many questions, God finally had made it clear that I had not gotten a book contract and Mary Beth had not gotten a child with cancer because *either* of us deserved it (she was so very glad God was there to see them all through the ordeal!), I still struggled with a small, stubborn sense of guilt. Exactly who was I and where was God taking me? Needing peace in this troubled corner of my heart, I stopped walking and called aloud toward the ocean. "Lord, who do you say that I am? You need to tell me. *Who do you say that I am?*" Tears and a sense of urgency caused my voice to rise and compete with the great roar before me. It did not seem an unfair question; even Christ had asked it of his disciples (Matthew 6:15). Of course that was their test, not his. But his words coming out of my mouth did not seem inappropriate.

And then I heard God's voice. Clearly God's voice boomed in my head. "I AM" was all God said.

"Lord, that's not what I asked you. Who do you say that *I* am?" The words choked out of me, though I feared to be so bold as to answer back. To holler back to a God who was clearly talking to me. But Jacob wrestled with an angel an entire night until the angel blessed him, so I took a deep breath and unabashedly repeated my question: "Lord, that is not what I asked you. Who do you say that I am?"

"I AM. That is all you need to know." This came with a tone of finality; and then God's voice was silent. All I could hear now were the crashing, thunderous waves.

I stood staring at the gray horizon as it disappeared and reappeared between swells. Weeping. Finally understanding that God was all. God was all of me. God was all I needed to know, although I could never know all of God.

Moses once asked God, "Who am I, that I should go to Pharaoh and bring the Israelites out of Egypt?"

And God said, "I will be with you" (Exodus 3:11–12). It was all Moses needed to know. But he still asked more.

Moses said to God, "Suppose I go to the Israelites and say to them, 'The God of your fathers has sent me to you,' and they ask me, 'What is his name?' Then what shall I tell them?"

God said to Moses, "I AM WHO I AM. This is what you are to say to the Israelites: 'I AM has sent me to you.'"

I AM. God is everything. God is all we need to know when we can't seem to know anything else. God is everything and everything is God's, including the parts of me I so pridefully and stubbornly try hard to hang on to.[1]

❄❁❄

I once read a quote that said, "Some years have questions and some years have answers," to which I would add, "And some years have questions *and* answers, but not necessarily the answers to the questions asked." The truth is that questions engage our ability to sort and process, define and stretch, multiply and pinpoint. Seeking answers engages our faith. Good, pressing questions connect us with brilliant minds, as illustrated by how often we Google a question or read a biography of someone whose courage or actions we want to emulate. How many years of the game show *Jeopardy!* have winning contestants been winners for expressing the right question, which is, of course, also the answer?

Wow! Think about that! Perhaps *your* question is the answer, too! Maybe if, after we address our question to God, or to our friend or the dog, we then asked ourselves, Why *am I asking that question?* we would dig up enough deep information to discover that we already *know* the answer. Which frees us to move on to our next question. Or to box with God about an answer we don't like. And I'm here to tell you, I have boxed with God! I have swung away, air-punching and flailing until I've melted to the ground in my own worn-out puddle. And you know what God says after *that* kind of show?

God comes to my puddle of a pathetic self and says, "I AM still here, child of mine."

✸ ✿ ✸

I now have the answer to which of the remaining eight women on the card I want to be: I want to be the one who's remembered as someone who really lived. From the looks of things, I'd say since all nine of these woman had the guts to say yes to running in a pack while flipping pancakes, laughing all the way to wherever they were going, they *all* surely did—at least for a moment in time. Make me any one of them, aside from number three, who is already taken, of course.

Who among them would have ever guessed that in that moment of a shutter snap, which they might have had no idea even took place, all these decades later and at *this* very moment in time, another woman, a woman who has no idea who they even are, would study their faces and whisper "thank you" to them and that others would be reading *her* story?

Now, there is a question that begs more questions, like, How many of *our* moments will others remember decades from now? What are we doing to make a difference in their lives?

Will my granddaughters remember their Grannie B with a smile on her face? Or will George snap a picture of me when I'm whirling in my office chair screaming *"WHAT?!"* And might *it* one day end up on a greeting card with a caption that says, "Happy Grandparents' Day, you old hag!"?

❖✿❖

Yup. We want answers, and now. Perhaps if we examine why we're asking the question (like, how will my grandchildren remember me?), we'll already know the behavior that needs to change, so we'll *stop* asking the question and start working on a remedy.

Or, at other times, we may just need to rest in unknowing as we cling to hope, sharpen our faith, and rekindle a few of life's *non*-instant processes, like handwritten prayer journals. There, after we ask the question and answers or bubbles of insight come, we record them. This way we won't forget how many questions we *do* receive answers for. As quickly as time flies, we want to be awake when those answers come.

❖✿❖

Our lives on this earth pass so quickly. In a castanetting finger snap, Mar and I are now the old ladies, although there are certainly those who are older. We occasionally joke about what it will be like when we're in the home. Mar wants me to promise to bring her strands of beads she can finger, play with, and wear. Me, well, if I go to the home first and she brings *me* beads, I just hope I don't eat them.

10 * decorating with rocks and rockets

Awakening Our Senses

Now that you're awake and leaning on your friends, have learned to laugh at yourself, challenge your assumptions, and utter encouraging inner talk, consider your questions, loosed your lean, and are paying attention to "Beware!" signs when you feel a SPLAT charging your way (pant-pant, inhale—slowly exhale), let us consider a gentle soothing art that can help us keep our balance. It's one that can remind us of who we are, whence we came, and where we want to go or stay.

Although some might say I live with my head in the clouds (I hear you, my dear brother-in-law), I often have my eyes to the ground since I am an earth person. Oceans and giant lakes are nice, but I prefer the craggy view of a windswept bluff, a forest thick with the fragrance of pine, a creek alive with crawdads, or a mile-long furrow of rich black earth. Because of this, on my entryway table sits a foot-long, six-inch-wide, shallow, rustic hand-carved (more like recklessly hand-gouged) wooden bowl that I purchased many years ago for a buck at a garage sale. It serves as my depository for miscellaneous things I run across and later extract from my pocket or suitcase. These simple objects are tokens, remnants, and reminders of a good day, time, walk, or friend. Like a sparrow scouting the ground for things with which to build its messy nest, so, too, am I drawn to sundry earthen things with which to surround myself. Things such as silvery sparkling rocks, quartets of acorns, slivers of weather-worn barn siding, a pinch of freshly mown hay, interesting twigs, or a found

penny, which, if it's dirty enough, also ends up in the bowl.

I study this collection of my finds and realize I no longer remember where most of them came from, can't tell one acorn from the next or one year's deposit from the other. But it doesn't matter, since look at all the places I've been! They are sacred, these icons of a life lived outside these walls, this block, myself. I rest my palm on top of them as if to feel Mother Earth speak to my fingertips through them: *Thank you for remembering me.*

I've stood in a kitchen at the estate sale of a stranger clutching the family cookbook with hand-scrawled recipes for "Aunt Mabel's chocolate cake," "sister Ethel's rhubarb pie," "Uncle Hank's beer brats," and "Mom's fried chicken" tucked inside. I flip through the pages as tenderly as if I were brushing an eyelash from my granddaughter's eyelid, and I weep. My memory portfolio is so enriched and brought to life by these types of treasures from my own life. Is there none left in this family who will be the keeper of the recipes, who knows the stories that go along with them? Who were these men and woman, *really?* What color were their eyes? Did they have no daughters or sons who liked to cook, sons like mine (bless you, boys) who telephone for recipes, ask me to write them down, or sort through my cookbooks when they're home for a visit? Perhaps not. Or perhaps it's just that no one in that family has yet considered the pieces of their past—flavor, smells, memories of gatherings around the table where these tasty and sometimes disastrous dishes were served up—that bind them together and that are now about to float away. Or maybe the person whose estate I picked through was the last in the family line. [MOMENT OF TRUTH: It just crossed my mind that maybe their cooking was so consistently horrid that their cookbooks were intentionally shunned, but that's not my point here.]

For years after my mother died, I wondered what happened to her recipe for My Man's Cookies. At least that's what I remembered her calling those delicious treats. My mom was a good cook. She made the best fried chicken and mashed potatoes covered with white gravy, and pineapple cream pie, and . . . But this cookie recipe haunted me. Where had it gone? After I wrote about it in *The 12 Dazes of Christmas (& One Holy Night)*,[1] a kind reader sent me the recipe, said she'd had it for years, surmised it was the same one. I made them and they sure tasted like it! But you see, only four months after my mother's sudden death, my father remarried. He was lost, lonesome, devastated. He simply could not be alone. I understood. He married a previous stranger to him, a widow who brought her own set of family memories and cookbooks into the house. Since my dad lived half a country away, and since, although he loved to cook, he didn't bake—and since I wasn't clearheaded enough to think about it until it was too late—nearly all my mom's cookbooks and hand-tucked recipes disappeared.

Perhaps that explains some of my tears over the recipes of people I don't even know. Sometimes I try one of them and shoot up a prayer of gratefulness for their handwritten memento while it's baking.

Cookbooks. Old family photos. Pieces of dishware. Articles of clothing. Yellowed diaries. Newspaper clippings. A hand-hewn wooden bowl filled with pieces of earth, each a reminder of a life lived, perhaps the life of someone who's gone before us, paved the way for us to draw this moment's breath so that we can exhale and speak their stories into the next generation.

❋ ❋ ❋

One day I looked out our kitchen window and witnessed the wrecking ball swinging into the side of the grammar school across the street, the one our sons attended. Our sons, the sons and daughters of others before them, and before them. All those years I'd listened to that happy laughter and schoolyard yelling, heard the bell, watched the kids pour forth, felt their joy at the end of the day, papers in their hands, backpacks thumping against their lungs, and now this.

I phoned my oldest son. "Bret, the wrecking ball's over at Spalding School." Desperate to remember it before it was even gone, I pleaded, "Tell me a story! What do you remember from your days at Spalding?"

Without skipping a beat, he said, "Do you know what I remember, Mom? I remember makin' eights."

"Making eights?"

"Yes. The teacher made us draw them in one continuous motion." My mildly rebellious "chip off his mildly rebellious mama's block" son, said, "That's why I make them with two circles today." Imagine, more than three decades later, my son remembers a quickened moment in time of makin' eights!

I hung up and phoned Brian. "Brian, the wrecking ball's over at Spalding. Tell me a story. What do you remember? Bret remembers makin' eights."

He can tell I've been crying. "Mom, is this a menopause thing?"

"No, Brian! It's about Spalding School and all the memories they're smashing down. Tell me a story."

"Here's something. I remember walking down the hall in a new pair of blue corduroy pants and the sound they made when I walked."

Wonders! Slices of lives! Chock-full memory portfolios! Makin' eights. The sound of blue corduroy pants.

I realized that I, too, have a quickened memory from my grammar school days. The teacher is pointing to a glass of melted snow she's placed on the windowsill. She asks us to closely inspect it in the sunlight so we can see the particles of dirt, which is supposed to (HA!) keep us from licking it off the handrails, our palms, or the ground when our faces smash down in it as we roll out of our snow angels.

What's odd to me is that I can *still* smell that schoolroom. Even though it wasn't the *same* school, it smelled the same as the now-missing Spalding School. What *is* it about that smell, that even if we were blindfolded and led through a twenty-mile obstacle course to get there, we would immediately recognize ourselves to be in a grammar school by that *smell*?! And *oh*, the memories it invokes!

✳ ✻ ✳

STOP READING! Take a moment to sift for one of your grammar school memories—although I bet it already made itself known by the mere thought of that smell.

❋ ❋ ❋

Sensory-laden memories. A whiff of a fragrance that brings to mind a past lover, rain on a highway, or a bakery in France. The pleasing sight of the cowlick on a newborn's crown located just where yours swirls, or a sweet lemonade reminiscent of a visit to the state fair. That *song*. We are a sensory-loaded people. Life is happening all around us; each sensuous experience capable of reminding us of another. Icons. Touchstones.

Transporters.

Antiques that remind us how far all the generations before us have evolved . . . or how far away we've wandered from a basic, sturdy hand-hewn wooden bowl that speaks of craft and contentment. In our striving to get ahead in terms of rank and position, income and better stuff, sometimes we end up further behind in terms of our sanity and peace, time and relationships—simply because we forget to pay attention to our senses.

Wake up.

Wake up your senses, again and again and again.

❋ ❋ ❋

I once read a quote on a billboard in front of a rental place: NATURE IS A GLOVE ON THE HAND OF GOD. Wow! Talk about awakening your senses!

Imagine.

Imagine stepping onto a soft moss-laden path that winds into the heartbeat of a damp forest. It's twilight, just enough light to illuminate your way and just enough darkness to cause you to look harder, listen more carefully. You hear, slightly to your left, what sounds to be a creek somewhere in the distance. You're thirsty, so you follow the happy gurgle, yet stay mindful of your steps. A gentle breeze crosses your forehead, delivers the scent of . . . honeysuckle? You drink, then relax, take off your shoes, feel the inviting earth beneath your toes. ("Walking barefoot in grass makes your understanding tingle," my friend says.[2]) You nap, then awaken to the bright light of the full-faced man in the moon beaming down on you. There's an elegant long-necked deer just off to your left.

Imagine.

Never . . . hurry.

Stay awake enough to notice what's around you.

However, whether imagined or happening in real time, not all sensory-laden experiences in our MPs start off with pleasant enticement.

* ❊ *

When the funeral director handed me a plastic bag containing my father's personal effects gathered from the hospital, included in them was his thin wallet. The leather was worn smooth and it smelled of him. It bore a familiar and heavenly, fragrant blend of leather, machine-shop oil, a tinge of bowling alley, a trace amount of hand soap, and a dab of fresh air. Since I live mostly in jeans, for quite a while after my father's death, I used it as my wallet just so I could take it out of my back pocket and drink of that sorely missed scent of my father. Then one day I went to retrieve it, and it was gone!

The last place I remembered using it was that very morning after breakfast out with my friend. We ate at a nearby IHOP, I paid my share, slid the wallet into my back pocket, and came home. Later, while running errands, I readied to pay the dry cleaners and found no wallet. I frantically raced back to IHOP, searched the booth we sat in, the floor, the parking lot, lost and found, then I searched them all again. The restaurant's staff searched everywhere with me. No wallet. I left my name and phone number and cried all the way home. I phoned my girl-friend. Had she noticed anything about the wallet that morning? Only that I'd used it; I was not insane. Where could it have gone? I searched my car and my house as I wept. I beat myself up. *I am so careless with my belongings! I've always been careless! WHY was I carrying Dad's wallet around!* I recalled all the beautiful pieces of jewelry I'd lost, including several my father gave me. My husband spends his life looking for my glasses. But losing this wallet, this potent, sensory-laden connection with my father, was my worst careless loss of all.

Later in the afternoon I went into our bathroom and . . . *Oh my gosh!* I couldn't believe what I was seeing! A corner of the wallet was stuck between the porcelain bowl and the toilet seat while the rest of it hung out in front of it, as if the toilet were sticking its tongue out at me. *Oh!* It's *here!* I laughed, I cried . . . but before I touched it, I went and got the camera and took a picture of it. I wish I could show it to you right here, but the best I can do is to send you back to www.dontmissyourlifebook.com. The shot was taken with an old Polaroid (pre-digital-camera days) still loaded with old film, so it's not too great, but I used that camera to make sure I'd captured this unbelievable sight. I laughed and I cried some more. My dad would have loved this story!

The best I can figure is that earlier, when I'd used the toilet, the gap between the bowl and the lid snagged the corner of the wallet and pulled it out of my back pocket. Then again, perhaps my dad talked to God and the two of them figured a way to play a good trick on me. Either way, I keep the photo displayed in my office to remind me that what's lost *is* sometimes found and who's gone is never forgotten.

I no longer carry the wallet. I feared if I carried it much longer, Dad's wonderful scent would be overshadowed by my love for perfume. I keep it in an old wooden toolbox that still smells like my dad, along with his driver's license and a few other trinkets from his life. Like memory-grabbing tentacles, my senses look at, then lift and smell the leather as I recall so many instances of my dad's loving hands guiding me through my life.

I remember rocking Bridget until she went limp in my arms, her little head resting against my chest. I couldn't even think about putting her down in the crib, so wonderful was the moment. I quietly sang. I nuzzled my nose against her silky hair. Nearly three hours later, there we still were. When I babysit my granddaughters, I'm told they often seem to nap longer than usual. I like to tease my son and daughter-in-law that it's the patchouli fragrance I wear, which is actually only one of the scents in an inexpensive blend of patchouli, ylang-ylang, and myrrh I have specially mixed for me at a little boutique shop not too far from home. My son shakes his head, smiles, or acts like he disapproves, since patchouli has so often been associated with the hippie generation, whose many wild and "free love" experiences I somehow missed.

But I wonder, will my granddaughters one day catch a waft of patchouli and remember me, long after I've left this earth? Might they smile and say, "I still miss my Grannie B"?

I hope so.

Take a look around your home, your office, your car, inside your handbag. Even though you might be one of those clutter-free types, surely you have some touchstones to your past, your loved ones, your earthy or oceanly self, don't you? If you don't, perhaps it's time to plant a small garden of reminders.

If you have too many of them, so many that they're lost in the chaos of one another, do a little sorting, a little tucking away, perhaps even a lot of giving away. Just don't forget to accompany each touchstone to the pieces of your life with a prayer of thanksgiving for the memory.

Look.

Hear.

Taste.

Touch.

Smell.

Drink of life using every sensual gift God has given you.

"*leap and the net will appear

Risking, Relishing, and Faith

Most new adventures ("Hey, *Don't Miss Your Life!*" "Okay!") are launched by passionate drivers extracted from our "golf" bags for life. Of course we carry our emotional putters and three woods, sand wedges, and ball retrievers to help get us out of predicaments. But oh, how we love pulling out that passionate driver. How else would, *could*, we launch our new pluck-and-play approach to live life to the full?! We've worked at—and worked out—everything else on our checklist. Now we're teed up on the icons that remind us of our heritage and have lined up the shot toward our dreams. *Right on!* Just like the pros, we've warmed up with a waggle or two. *Oh, baby, get ready!* We imagine the most magnificent trajectory. *I can visualize my attempt hitting the mark.* However, the catch is this: we're still listening to a teensy-tiny bit of our negative thinking. "What if I fail? What if I hit my best shot out of bounds?" As long as we postpone activating that big-boy driver, we don't have to *risk* failing at our goals, dreams, whims, or heart's desire. *YIPPIE!* Unless of course we die before seeing our dreams come to fruition, which is likely to happen if we're unwilling to get off the tee and take a leap of faith. *Ding-dong!*

~~~~~~

The tragedy of life is what dies inside

a man while he lives.

ALBERT SCHWEITZER

~~~~~~

"But what if I take that leap of faith and I *do* fail, Charlene? Don't act like that isn't possible!" To which I respond, of *course* it's possible. Sure, you might look like a fool. People might scoff, run film clips of your sorry disaster on the five o'clock news. Even make fun of your hair while they're gossiping about your cumulative *past* financial risks and failed attempts.

My contention, as well as that of many experts, is this: What matters more than a failure is how you respond to it. Will you bounce back? Lie there in defeat? Parlay the wisdom you could receive only through failure into your next great attempt? Disappear into seclusion? Recircle your wagons, bring in an expert, tweak your theme, change the target a tad, and have at it again? Poke out your eye? Cry . . . but toast to your next attempt tomorrow morning?

This I know to be true about me: I'd rather risk failure than live with the knowledge I never tried. If you stifle your dreams and goals because you're afraid to take a risk, is that not like pinching off the blooms of possibility until you at long last strangle the life out of your own vine?

ACTIVATE!

✻❇✻

We (read I) purchased a new object of art I wanted to display. "George, can you please hang this on the wall behind the couch?"

"How high do you want it?"

"Oh, you know, about eye level." George is six one and I'm five three and a half, which of course begs George, the engineer, to ask *whose* eye level? "Somewhere in the middle," I respond. Easy. He's looked down at me (not in that way) so long that he should be able to split the difference. *Hello!* All he need do is eyeball the wall with his own eyeballs, picture me standing there against the wall, then point his finger in the middle of those two heights. Plus, there's the couch, and the obvious middle of *it* would be halfway through the center cushion. He shouldn't need me for this task, so I wander off to do something else.

Later, I pass through the living room and note the object of art is still in a chair. George has a tape measure, a calculator, slide rule, level, twenty sizes of nails, and other hang-it-up-and-on implements and two types of hammers. Okay, I'm exaggerating, but he has way more tools and has taken way more time than I deem necessary for this simple task. I say a few encouraging words [MOMENT OF TRUTH: likely not] as I remind him about all the *other* things still on the "honey do" list. He looks at me (a glance, really), nods, and goes back to drawing some kind of schematic.

The next time I pass through the room, the object is still in one chair and George now sits in another chair, his chart or schematic or what by *now* must surely be a diagram of THE ENTIRE UNIVERSE AND EVERYTHING IN IT on his lap, pencil skittering this way and that. I can't take it anymore. I grab the hammer, a nail, give the wall a squinty eyeball. (Hear George yelling in the background, something about studs, or molly bolts, or . . .) A short amount of time after my four *whap-whap-whap-whaps*, the nail is in the wall and the object of art is in place. "There!" I say. "I wanted it *there* and now you can move on to the next thing."

Before you start cheering my valiant ability to activate, to grab my passionate driver and smack that ball off the tee, ask yourself this question: aren't you glad I don't build bridges? You *should* be! Sometimes a gross amount of calculating and planning is necessary. [MOMENT OF TRUTH: Once, when Bret was home for a visit, he looked at three pictures hanging in a row on the kitchen wall near the table. "You hung these, didn't you, Mom?" Of course every single one of them was callywhompus, so of *course* I'd hung them. How did I raise such a smarty-pants?!]

There is a time and place for spontaneous activation and a time for calculated planning. We have a need for thinkers and a need for doers. We learn from our great ponderers (bless your Daily Ponderables, Al Harris!) and yet are grateful for those who nudge us to give something a try ourselves.

Stand back and try to gain some perspective on what you need at this time in your life. If you're feeling stuck in your rut or lost to your soul, or hear the clock ticking on that window of opportunity, perhaps it's time to get out that passionate driver and just *blammo!*

✳❋✳

Since the first time I witnessed someone bungee jump, I wanted to do it. I longed to feel that maiden tilting rush, experience the screaming drop, then the powerful *boing* that snaps you up from the jaws of peril. But I was sure the fun wouldn't end there: the tension between the pull of gravity and the bungee cord would undoubtedly drop me down again and *boing* me up again, repeating until I'd once again settle on the ground. Gently, of course. Hopefully.

When Brian was still in college, during a bungee-jumping fund-raiser, George and I once watched him bungee jump. I have wonderful pictures of his ascent, him looking over the edge, his spread-eagle dive into thin air, the slack in the bungee cord when he looped back up as if connected to a big umbilical cord in the sky. His ticket was purchased ahead of time, all the slots were filled, and we were there to observe. This day was for college kids. But one day, *I* would get my opportunity, wouldn't I?

Shortly thereafter—and still during the height of the bungee craze—my Kiwanis group was scouting for fund-raising opportunities and I begged them to consider such an event. (Hey, if you can't get to the bungee, bring the bungee to you!) I got nowhere. There was talk of liabilities and several bungee deaths that had recently made national news. I was overruled. No bungee for me. And then the craze passed, traveling bungee gigs disappeared, and other things came along. But the bungee gods continued to whisper my name.

Fast-forward many years and step into my drama as, with the help of my MP, I relieve it.

I no longer belong to Kiwanis. I am much older. I've experienced back problems and neck issues and I take blood-pressure medication. I am overweight, own no motorcycles (haven't for decades), nearly ditched a moped, and am still married to George, who doesn't encourage risk. His idea of high adventure: riding the Original Wisconsin Ducks,[1] those crazy "amphibious (land/water) vehicles with six driving wheels, a steel hull and the capacity to carry 25 people on land or 50 people while afloat and 5,000-pounds of general cargo." Yes, the same vehicle can and does putter along on both land and water, and we can take a ride in it. "Original Wisconsin Ducks has an exemplary safety record with 57 years of operation in Wisconsin Dells." Oh boy. Yawn.

In fairness, I *do* enjoy the Original Wisconsin Ducks, mostly since they wash up fun memories of doing the Dells as a child, plus I like the Wisconsin River, and I also like George. *Plus*, they sell wonderful fudge at the Wisconsin Dells. Mmm. So off we go. We two wild things get so crazy, we (read me) decide we'll even get a room and stay a night or two rather than make the 2.5-hour drive home after the exhilarating (yawn) land/water extravaganza. We can call it a minivacation, George! *Hear George sigh*.

After our high adventure, but before we head back to the motel, George asks me if there's anything else I'd like to do. "I'm not sure. Turn right up there," I say, striving to sound casually normal [MOMENT OF TRUTH: I'm trying to hide something from him], which I'm not, but again let me remind you that George is used to me by now, so he turns.

"Where are we going?" he asks.

"I thought I saw something on our way here and I just want to check it out."

"What?"

"I'll tell you when and if I see it," which is about when the banner appears. "Turn in up there where the sign says 'Extreme World.'"[2] And so he does, and then he sees what I'm looking at, which is a person falling from the sky, headfirst. George looks at

me out of the corner of his suddenly concerned eye. "I just want
to watch," I say. He pulls the car into a parking spot facing away
from the *boing*ing bungee jumper. I get out, lean back against the
back bumper of the car, and watch and wait until said person, a
teen boy, is deposited back onto the earth.

George remains behind the wheel, spying on me in his rearview mirror. (Guess who he learned *that* from?) He starts the
engine. "Ready to go?" he asks through his open window, a hopeful yet firm note in his voice.

"Not yet. I see another young kid getting ready. Come on, get
out of the car. Let's go up there and watch." The bungee landing
is up on a hill. George announces he's *ready to go*, but I'm already
walking away from him toward my target. (Feel me teeing up?)

"Come on!" I shout over my shoulder. "I just want to *watch*!"

Reluctantly, he locks the car (and checks all the doors to make
sure they're locked, which is his traveling mantra: security first!)
and follows me to a picnic table near the landing pad where we take
a seat. We're now within listening range of the man I shall refer
to as Bungee Master. The new rider, a wiry young boy, is in the
cage (they call it a bogey car) that will lift both the boy and Bungee
Master thirteen stories up (tallest bungee jump in the state of Wisconsin: 130 feet) before it stops. The boy listens intently as Bungee
Master delivers his repeated-many-times-a-day instructions.

"When we stop at the top, I will open the gate and you will
step to the edge of the opening. You will stretch both hands out
in front of you, palms together. When you feel my hand on your
back, you just lean forward until you fall out." (Did I mention this
place uses an *ankle* harness?)

"Once you're falling, you can do anything you want, but do not
attempt to grab the cord or the cage." In other words, once committed, don't try to change your mind or you might accidentally
hang yourself, split your head into pieces, or rip your arms out of

their sockets. Or tip the cage, causing Bungee Master, who wears no bungee cords, to fall out. At least that all sure looks possible to *me*. There's a few moments of repeating the expected drill, and then, up they go. My heart races as I "feel" the jolt when the cage begins to lift. I hold my hand over my eyebrows to shield my eyes from the sun. I watch, wait, hold my breath. Then the cage stops, the gate opens, and the boy does as he was told. Down he dives, screaming all the while. But when he gets to the bottom of the bungee cord, which is a long way above the ground, he barely snaps back up. He barely bounces at all before coming to a stop and getting lowered to the ground. I hear one of the ground-floor bungee workers say to a fellow worker, "Well, *that* was a terrible ride, but the guy doesn't weigh enough for a better one." I look at my girth and think, *Now, I would have a good ride, wouldn't I?*

"Okay, let's go," George says. But I notice a man is gearing up to go next. A grown man. A midlife man.

"Let's watch one more," I say.

"Come on," George nearly demands, sensing trouble closing in on his dearly beloved.

"No. I want to watch this guy." While they're hooking him up, I stand up on the seat bench of the picnic table and hold my hands out in front of me. I close my eyes, imagine myself thirteen stories high, *imagine* leaning forward. George is standing now, too, all but grabbing my hands and dragging me to the car, which he knows he'll have to do to get me to leave. He sees the lure of this opportunity in my eyes. Although I am not committed, he thinks I am. This is a risky thing to do at any age. Perhaps my window of opportunity counted down years ago and I just didn't notice, but I need to stay at least long enough to figure it out.

Perhaps I *don't* have the guts.

The woman watching her bungee-jumping man stands near our table to take it all in. I ask her if he's done this before and she says no, but that he's always wanted to. She's smiling, kind of, yet she slams her hand over her mouth as she watches him go up, up, up . . . and then dive down, down, down—*BOING!* We audibly hear her relief. She takes a step toward his exit gate and I hear myself blurt, *"Wait!* Would you mind waiting here for him so I can hear what he has to say?"

"Not at all!"

"Let's go!" George says, his face stern.

"Not yet! I want to listen to a firsthand account!"

The man walks toward us. He appears slightly unsteady but he is grinning from ear to ear. And then he breathes a breath of resolve into my core. "Well, I can die now and say I *did* it!"

That's all I need to hear. Since I've been watching, thinking back on all the bungee-lusting years, how many people I told I *wanted* to jump—never when there was an opportunity to do so, however—something bigger than actually experiencing the fall has now surfaced: a monster of a rash of questions. Would I, *could* I, still find the *nerve* to do it? To challenge myself to step into nothingness? To test my moxie? And if not now, when?

I empty my pockets of everything but the credit card and tell George I'm just going to go check out the prices. "Let's *go!*" he orders, giving me one more sensible chance to listen to him, to obey him, to respond to the pleading look in his eyes, which I don't. And yet, all the while I'm walking to the ticket place, which is quite a ways from the actual bungee jump, I am thinking, *I'm too old. I'm too overweight. What if I wrench my back? George is probably right. We should probably go.* But my feet keep taking the next step and my mind won't stop replaying, *If not now, when? Test yourself, Charlene!*

I can die and say, "I DID IT!" Yea, baby!

But will I?

Can I look my mounting fear in the face and stare it down?

There are warning signs posted all around. IF YOU HAVE BACK

PROBLEMS . . . IF YOU HAVE HEART DISEASE . . . But my back's been fine lately. Besides, the bungee ropes stretch and *boing* you back up, not slam-bang *jerk* you. And taking high-blood-pressure medications doesn't mean you actually have heart disease, does it? The little gal at the counter says she cannot answer medical questions. She pushes a wad of papers in front of me that I must sign, which say it won't be their fault if I die.

No, if I die, it will be on account of my own pigheadedness and stupidity or, moreover, my own need to feel alive, trusting, and brave enough to overcome my own hesitancy—my need to not let fear stop me. *A worthy goal!*

The inner turmoil is bubbling. I don't realize how tightly wound I've become, how nervous—dare I say scared?—until I start signing my name and only scribble ends up on the paper. *I cannot even recognize my own name,* my hand is trembling so badly. But still, I taunt myself like the schoolyard bully. *Bock-bock-bock. Chicken liver.*

Do not listen to the voice of fear, Charlene! You'll regret saying no to this window of opportunity—possibly your last—for the rest of your days.

George sits at the picnic table, elbows resting on the surface, his face buried in his hands. I know he is praying. I hand him my credit card along with the receipt. He rolls his eyes at the price. *Whatever I've paid for this opportunity, it's worth it.* I secure my T-shirt with a makeshift knot. I've watched how *boing*ing forces combined with hands over a head duplicate the old skin-the-cat game we used to play with the kids. Heaven forbid I should bungee without decorum. [MOMENT OF TRUTH: Apparently, decorum strikes me as important when I think I'm going to die with my flabby stomach hanging out.]

I'm hoping I don't have to wait for anyone else to go, which would allow more time for me to bail, but during my decorum attack someone else jumps in line in front of me. *Dang decorum!*

My heart's pounding so loud I imagine everyone around me can hear it. While one bungee worker finishes preparing the guy in front of me (the fruit of my decorum folly), another starts with me. He begins by asking me how much I weigh, which doesn't seem like a good time to lie since a person's weight is what determines the number of bungee cords (or thickness of the one, or whatever) it will take to prevent a face-plant. I tell him, and then he has me walk to a scale—which I had somehow missed before I bought my ticket. I briefly wonder if knowing *this* might have influenced my decision. Before I'm done wondering, he has me step to a second scale; then he YELLS my weight to a guy out there somewhere.

This is where I momentarily fear for *George's* life, the shock of the reality of my weight perhaps too much for him to bear.

Then they have me sit down so they can bind my ankles together with the straps to which my lifelines will be attached. *Velcro!* (I'm sure there were safety straps around the Velcro, too, but I don't remember them.) I sit there with my legs bound together, feeling like I might hyperventilate, watching the young man before me go up in the cage. I glance down and notice that my toes are turning blue, about which I inquire.

"Would you like me to loosen the straps?" the guy asks.

"NOOOOOO!"

He smiles, obviously not the first time he's asked the question and witnessed the guaranteed hysterical answer.

I feel like I might be sick after the guy in front of me tumbles from the sky and I hear the cage clank down into place—the cage that will take me thirteen floors over my head, which, from this perspective, looks to be close to heaven. Bungee Master says it's time I get in. I look at my bound ankles and ask, "How?" He coaxes me to just scoot over any way I can, which I do by swinging my toes, then my heels, toes, heels, toes, heels until I arrive at the cage's edge and notice it's about six to eight inches above my feet. "Just hop up," he says, seeing I've paralyzed myself.

This is where I'm going to die! In one daredevil move I'm going to have to risk heaving my entire fluffy body into the air and land it eight inches up and over there. If I miss, I'll go down, hit my head on the metal, and that will be that.

I am risking death.

I glance down at what looks to be the air mattress where I'll ultimately land (*Please, God!*) and think, *Yes, you're risking death, Charlene. Is this worth it?*

You will not *chicken out, do you* hear *me?* I muster my resolve and in one svelte leap I manage to make it into the cage. Bungee Master congratulates me, asks me to move to the side of the cage, then begins to give me the instructions.

"Now, when the cage stops at the top, I will open the gate and you will step to the edge of the opening. You will stretch both hands out in front of you, palms together. When you feel my hand on your back, you just lean forward until you fall out." He goes on to repeat the warning about not trying to grab the cage or the bungee cords. Fat chance, I think. I'll probably pass out the moment I feel that hand on my back.

He hollers my weight again, which is acknowledged back to him. With a lurch, up we start to go. Immediately I close my eyes.

"You have your eyes closed already? This isn't a good sign," Bungee Master says. "Just so you know, once we get to the top, you can still change your mind, but you won't get your money back."

"It's not about the money, and I won't change my mind," I say to him and myself. I've opened my eyes to speak, which is a big mistake. Me, the wild-child horse-and-motorcycle-riding daredevil, suddenly goes weak in the knees. (Thank goodness I didn't have that moped experience before this opportunity. I'm sure I'd never have attempted to bungee after that!) I've heard people de-

scribe this moosh-leg sensation before and thought, *What wimps*.
Now I get it; it feels like my rubbery legs might stop holding me
up. Bungee Master is again repeating the instructions. I'm striving to concentrate, to visualize what will take place—to will myself
to do as I am told when it's time, even though my eyes are again
closed. The cage jars to a halt, as does my breath.

"You have to open your eyes now," he says, so I do. *GASP!* I can't
believe how high we are. My legs are pure pudding. I'm afraid I'm
going to faint or have a heart attack. He opens the gate, which
COMPLETELY FREAKS ME OUT SINCE NOTHING IS HOLDING
US IN HERE NOW! "Okay, scoot to the edge, then grab ahold here
and then here," he says, showing me how to get into position, one
hand on each side of the opening. Toe, heel, toe, heel I scoot until
my arms are stretched out behind me as far as they will go. I need
to release my death grip on the rail behind me before I can grab
hold of what's on either side of that which is before me: nothing but sky. Honestly, letting go of that rail is almost paralyzing!
My heart, my legs . . . Only the *unacceptable* consequence of living
with the knowledge I chickened out enables—*forces*—me to get in
place.

"Okay, now put your hands out in front of you," which means
letting go of all security. I do it immediately before I have a chance
to talk myself out of it. Legs quaking, I clasp my hands in front of
me as if praying—which I don't have time to do before I feel his
hand on my back, which is the signal to lean forward, which I do.

The moment I feel my body fall into the dive position and my
feet leave the frame, while screaming my lungs out, I'm already
celebrating in my head. *I DID IT! I DID IT! I DID IT!*

I never once open my eyes on that first dive down, but I experience a giant crescendo of knowing within me that I know that
I *know* that no matter *what* happens next, I cannot fall out of the
safety net of *God's* arms! Seriously! That thought is in my mind as

I encounter my first giant *boing*ing snapback upward. I open my eyes on my second *boing* to watch the world float up and down in front of me. The video (yes, I bought it!) reveals that I never unclenched my prayer-clasped hands.

* ✿ *

I can die now and say I did it. I can move forward knowing I had the guts and the good sense to go after one of my goals, one of my dreams, while the window of opportunity stood wide open before me. I can die knowing I still have it in me to *face down fear*.

Oh, the continuous inspiring rush of knowing that my own fear did not conquer me! Just remembering this encourages me to rent me another moped. I shall open my MP and fly that joyful fear-squelcher flag in front of my face every time fear tries to sneak up on me again. Even if I'd *splatted*, I would have gone down celebrating. Rather than spending this moment typing, my mom and dad and I would still be swapping stories together in heaven, rejoicing in how fully we had *lived*!

* ✿ *

Life is important, risky, wondrous, baffling, fragile, exotic, and a surprise. As my friend Al Harris said in *another* of his marvelous Daily Ponderables, "All of life is a near-death experience."

Courage is resistance to fear,

mastery of fear—not absence of fear.

Mark Twain

What are you afraid of? What leap of faith (it doesn't have to be a literal leap like mine) might you courageously tee up with your passionate driver—then not talk yourself out of? What risk, the fulfillment of what dream, might the window of opportunity be open to right this minute? A new business venture? A vacation to a remote area? Match.com?

I once read a quote attributed to George Eliot that said, "It's never too late to become what you might have been." That is not only provocative but hope-filled and wise and can reinvigorate your personal resources when your old ones feel worn out or lost to the past.

Recently I've heard and read inspiring stories of people graduating from college in their late eighties and even their nineties. A college degree was always something to which they aspired but life's circumstances had kept them from it. Well, by golly, passion doesn't naturally wane just because we age. So if age is your excuse, get over yourself! Whether you're in your twenties or nineties, there are ways to accomplish your goals, to experience adventure, to try a new "course." Anything can be modified to suit your requirements. Listen to the stories of those who have gone before you. Let them awaken—reawaken—your goals and dreams you thought were gone forever.

Maybe it's time to invest in a new set of *mental* golf clubs designed for more flexible thinking. *Those* kinds of clubs will *surely* help you go the distance!

❖❀❖

What life pursuit do you hold back on because you've allowed fear a stranglehold rather than trusting God to see you through?

Have you forgotten that no matter how terribly you might fail, you can never fall out of the arms of God?

For I am convinced that neither death, nor life, nor angels, nor principalities, nor things present, nor things to come, nor powers, nor height, nor depth, nor any other created thing, will be able to separate us from the love of God, which is in Christ Jesus our Lord Romans 8:38 (NASB).

Whatever you want to do, do it now.

There are only so many tomorrows.

MICHAEL LANDON

Yes, this includes *failures*, so what are you waiting for? Leap and God's loving net—already in place—will appear before your very eyes!

12*imagine this!
A Mind's Ride to Play, Possibilities, and Change

"The longer I live the more I see how God often touches our lives through other people. I will never forget that magical autumn afternoon when He used Mr. Electrico to touch mine. It happened when I was 12, in my hometown of Waukegan, Illinois, on Lake Michigan's shore."

So begins word maestro Ray Bradbury's magnificent story "Mr. Electrico." If you haven't read it, do. Learn how one boy's encounter with a stranger in a traveling circus helps him to "Live forever"!

We have instruction manual upon instruction manual sitting all around us, help keys on our computers, "live" tech support online, and handheld gadgets to bind all of our facts together. We have planners to keep our appointments, e-mail to keep us posted, and consumer indexes to keep us depressed (*doink*). But what happens if we grab our passionate driver, ready to tee up our dream—and can't *find* a dream? What do we do when *possibility* thinking is required and that no longer seems possible? How do we get out of the box when we need to? Is *once upon a time* still even in our vocabulary? Has our sense of awe and wonder become dormant? Where, oh where, have our imagination and creativity gone? You know, that brilliant, God-given mind we were born with? The one I tried to warm up for you in the previous chapters? The one that could help us build blanket forts, Barbie relationships, and LEGO villages, become Superman by donning a bath towel, or be a real nurse to our rubber dollies? What happened to our imaginative ability to build our own real *dreams*? Our wizardly mind that helped us play with our thoughts long enough to ignite the magic?

Magic? You say you can't even *remember* the magic?

My friend Kayla (all names in this particular story changed to protect the innocent, the guilty, and . . . the magic) is a terrific businesswoman with a tender heart. She recently attended an all-day workshop presented by the Disney Institute of Leadership. "Trust me. When we got there, it was *all* about the magic!" she told this reporter during a recent interview, which was of course a disguised reason to do lunch. But since I thrive on the magical and the mystery, I couldn't wait to hear the details.

Kayla signed up for the workshop on the enthusiastic advice of a trusted friend who'd attended one of Disney's full-blown, five-day, on-site versions. Having experienced both Disneyland and Disney World herself, Kayla understood Disney's people-pleasing powers. Plus, she and her husband, Ben, had just taken their ten-year-old daughter, Stephanie, to Disney World. Her interest in the workshop was acute since a freshly captured "magical moment" still rode high in her consciousness.

Kayla defines a magical moment as "an unbelievably memo-

rable, captivating, totally engaging, sweet sensory experience."
(And I fancy myself the writer. Yowza!) Her recent magical
moment arrived during one of Disney's extraordinary light
shows. All day her family had romped together in the bountiful
world of wonder; this light-wielding wizardry offered yet more
dazzling frosting on a supersized castle cake. Her precise magical moment: not the light show itself, but a freeze-frame image
of her husband's and daughter's side-by-side profiles, faces to
the sky, eyes illuminated and wide with amazement at the sight
before them. Ben doesn't often let his guard down enough to
reveal the child within, so this moment was extramagical on several intimate levels. How could she not drool to attend a workshop put on by the very people who had set the stage for *that* entry
in her memory portfolio?

Kayla, an excellent storyteller, told me her personal takeaway
goals for the Disney workshop pertained to customer service:
"How do we make our company more client- or customer-
friendly?" Throughout the workshop she was struck by Disney's
unwavering behind-the-scenes attention to customer-service
details. The behavior and demeanor of everyone who works
for one of the Disney sites—from the parking attendants to the
ice-cream vendors to Mickey himself—are meticulously and
intently planned out with the ultimate goal of not only extending the magic but not killing it. An example she gave: you drop
your ice-cream cone on your first lick and they're dishing up
its free replacement as soon as they hear that familiar combo
crunch/splat. For customers to experience Disney's desires for
them, everything must also appear to be happening naturally,
organically, if you will, but oh, the intention with which that is
planned!

By the time Kayla's workshop day came to an end, she explained to me how she was *overflowing* with a sense of empower-

ment, chompin' at the bit to spread wonder and goodwill toward all. She whisked home with zeal in her heart and spontaneous imaginative plans to create a little magic for her family that very night. Yes, it was all about the staging, the behind-the-scenes efforts, going the extra mile to sprinkle a bit o' the pixie dust into the lives of those she loved. (She was lit up like a light show herself just telling me this part.) She not only cooked a special meal, but she *cleaned all the junk off the table* and put on a clean tablecloth. Oh boy! This was gonna be *great!*

You guessed it: one thing after the next went wrong and the slowing, plummeting tone in her storytelling voice directly matched each new detail of the slippery slide. The harder she'd tried to muster the magic, the more things didn't pan out the way she'd hoped. Her daughter rolled her eyes over the "special" food; Kayla strove to smooth the emotional bumps. Next came her daughter's whining about this and that, putting more nicks in Kayla's master magical plan. Eventually her husband asked Kayla why she was so . . . touchy that evening. Ultimately, she became so distressed—not only by her husband and daughter's lack of appreciation for her efforts but by their obvious shunning of what they didn't even *know* was supposed to be magical—that she finally and firmly spoke up. "I was just trying to do something *nice* here. I'm going to *leave* now before I say something I will regret." Out the door she disappeared.

People are just about as happy as

they make up their minds to be.

<small>ABRAHAM LINCOLN</small>

"The Magical Express that derailed" is how she put it. I laughed out loud here. What a great summation of her event. But wait, there's more.

She got in her car and started driving around to calm herself down. [MOMENT OF TRUTH: Boy, have I been *there*!] It was then her cell phone rang. She told me it was her sister calling with a routine check-in. What good or bad timing, depending on how you want to look at it. Kayla unloaded both barrels of her litany, starting with the workshop, slogging through every detail of magic run amuck, ending with her spinning car wheels. "I was just trying to create a little *magic*!" she sniveled to her sister, then repeated to me. I was *crazy* laughing by then, having recognized her most excellent description of what the universal descent into "derailment" truly sounded like.

When my laughter finally died down (I mean, she had me laughing so hard I was actually slapping the table while trying to catch my breath), I of course felt bad for Kayla on several counts, not the least of which was her relatable disappointment. As a mom, I know how that goes. Her story brought to mind the time (the only time) we decided to invite Bret's entire classroom full of kids to his birthday party in an attempt to create one of those fabulous magical memories. What a disaster! Nothing golden there; just a piñata that refused to break, unending chaos, kids bickering with one another . . . Truly, not a hint of magic, none whatsoever.

But even when I was laughing, the thing I felt the worst about for Kayla was the realization that spending the whole workshop day being reminded about the magic had left *her* longing to experience it. She yearned once again to be the *recipient* of a magical moment even if she had to create it herself—and who among us doesn't?

I know nothing with any certainty . . .

But the sight of stars makes me dream.

VINCENT VAN GOGH

When I think back on personal moments that still sparkle with the brilliance of life, I realize not one of them arrived because it was staged. Yes, I believe we can certainly help set the scene by slowing life down enough to *see* those magical moments (WAKE UP! and way to go, Disney!), but all in all, they will arrive when they will.

Magic happens.

Magic happens when, for unknown reasons, we capture a moment in a freeze-frame and tuck it in our MP, as I did while Kayla and I were laughing together. Such bright happy laughter shared by two longtime friends. I will never forget it.

Great guffawing laughter *is* magical. I need to call Kayla and let her know that she delivered after all!

✻ ❃ ✻

Albert Einstein said, "Imagination is more important than knowledge. Knowledge is limited; imagination encircles the world." I would add that imagination encircles—connects—way more than the worldly. Imagination enables us to reach "otherly" elements, perhaps even connecting with heaven. Then again, perhaps our own imagination, which I believe to be a gift from God, is one of the portals God uses to reach *us*, to give us those heavenly glimpses in order to keep us longing for him. Yes, perhaps

God created our imaginations as one of the least-suspecting ways to reach us through the Holy Spirit, communicate with us, allow us to "see" and "hear" more than we're able so that we don't freak out when we hear from God. Such was the following case for me.

❊ ❊ ❊

Opening time line: The end of a speaking engagement. I drove in last night, stayed at a hotel, checked out this morning, went and did my blabbing thing. I want to go home.

The location: Chesterton, Indiana, seventy-five miles from my home in Illinois, which is why I drove.

Obstacles: Interstate 80/94, one of the gnarliest, most highly truck-trafficked, and seemingly always "under construction" strips of roadway in the whole U.S. of A. I'm convinced of it.

Mental state: Tired, but good tired. Good tired, but nonetheless verging on running out of nice.

Bad news: A blizzard is sweeping in. Treacherous driving conditions. Stay off 80/94, George tells me. Drifts. Accidents. Warnings.

"Just stay there tonight. Be safe," my husband who loves me says. But I'm a cowgirl and a Gypsy at heart. I *know* I've already said this, but I used to ride in barrel races. I've owned two motorcycles. I'm dead tired and need my own bed since I've been on the road so much lately. What's a little snow to a *cowgirl*, George? But as usual, he's not buying it, and truthfully, I know he's right.

"Maybe they won't have a room," I say, my last-ditch attempt to defy anything reasonable, which, as you know by now, is often my default. But they do. The same one I occupied last night, in fact. With a very grumbling spirit, I drag my suitcase back out of the trunk. Even though I'm temporarily parked under the overhang, the side-winding wind and snow blades (that's what they feel like) lash at my face. I take my bag to my room, then come back down and park the car in the lot. I can't believe how much snow's already accumulated. By the time I get back to my room, I realize how bone weary I am, what a mistake it would have been to head out in this, and yet, I'm still ticked off. I grab a bite to eat (thank goodness the hotel has its own restaurant), go to bed early, and hurl myself into a very long bout of fitful tossing, turning, and juggling of unhappy thoughts before I finally nod off.

I awaken and open my eyes. Because the drapes in hotel rooms never seem to close quite all the way, the blinding slice of sunlight across my face lets me know it's morning. I look at the unfamiliar ceiling. *Rats! I'm still in Indiana!* Not that I don't love Indiana, I do. My dad was born and raised here. I have cousins whom I adore in this wonderful state. But right now I want to be home! I grumble and stomp my way to the window, pull back the blinds, and . . .

Oh! *OH!* The trees, the cars, the railing around my little balcony—everything—is blanketed with sparkling snow! Glimmering! Dazzling! More illuminated than diamonds under a jeweler's lamp! The sunlight makes the earth appear as if it were Cinderella's glittery ball gown, full flare, captivating the eye of not only the prince but the king of all creation. I wonder if God didn't put on this magnificent show for his *own* pleasure.

"See?" I hear God say to my heart. "*See* what you would have missed if you'd gone home last night?" *Yes.* My eyes are open. My pulse races. *Yes*, I say again. Imagining the earth as if it were Cinderella's fully billowing and sparking ball gown—a product of *another's* imagination—has opened my ears to hear more, my eyes to see more. *All* my senses are now fully ignited. I find I must—I cannot do anything other than—sit down at the little desk by the window, grab a paper and pen, and begin to write what I am hearing through my . . . imagination? Head? Heart? Whispers of the Holy Spirit?

LISTEN

Listen. Listen to Me. For Me. For My
Yes that frees you
to move and live
and breathe and dance in My Rhythm.

      Listen. Listen to Me. For Me. And I
      will tell you
      great and mighty things which you do not know.

Move. Move behind Me. Beside Me. And I
will sing you
to a new place of being.
A place where all you need to Be is
Listening.

      Move. Move behind Me. Beside Me. And I
      will take you to
      great and mighty places which you cannot imagine.

Embrace. Embrace Me to you. In you. And I
will impregnate you
with the seed
of holy bliss.

      Embrace. Embrace Me to you. In you. And I
      will spring forth as a
      great and mighty river within which you have not yet
        sailed.

Drink. Drink of Me. In Me. And I
will quench your
fear and sorrow
with heavenly brightness and healing.

> *Drink. Drink of Me. In Me. And I*
> *will rebirth you to a*
> *great and mighty place of peace.*

Listen. Move beside me.
Embrace me, gulp me down and I
will make you a
great and mighty heir to My kingdom of which you have not
> *even dared*
to dream.

> *Listen. Listen to me. For me.*
>> *I AM yours.*

When I finish writing this poem, I cannot discern the difference between my imagination, the creative process, and the voice of God, so triune and inseparable did they arrive. Cinderella's ball gown (imagination), "seeing" or "hearing" what had not heretofore existed and making it so (creation), "knowledge of" a great and mighty river within (God's promise).

~~~~~~

But when He, the Spirit of truth, comes,

He will guide you into all the truth;

for He will not speak on His own initiative,

but whatever He hears, He will speak;

and He will disclose to you what is to come.

He shall glorify Me; for He shall take of Mine,

and shall disclose it to you.

All things that the Father has are Mine;

therefore I said, that He takes of Mine,

and will disclose it to you.

JOHN 16:13–15 NASB

God within.

I am told God's sheep will hear God's voice and know it (John 10:27), Call me a poet, a creative listener, a woman with an enlivened imagination. But first call me a child of God, a child who occasionally—when the imagination is tuned to the right channel and the Holy Spirit has something to teach me—listens and hears.

Call me someone with no special powers unavailable to you.

* ❋ *

Imagine *this:* that imagination + creation + ears to hear (as in one of his sheep) is one of God's most unassuming methods to deliver all of that "disclosure" through the Holy Spirit.

In the Bible translation the Message, the Holy Spirit is referred to as the Friend. *But when the Friend comes, the Spirit of the Truth,*

*he will take you by the hand and guide you into all the truth there is.
He won't draw attention to himself, but will make sense out of what is
about to happen, and, indeed, out of all that I have done and said. He
will honor me, he will take from me and deliver it to you. Everything
the Father has is also mine. That is why I've said, "He takes from me
and delivers to you."*

"The Friend." Hmm. Remember your imaginary friend, how
well he or she knew you, how much she liked you? Notice in the
above passage how the Friend won't draw attention to himself
(*hmm!*), just like your imaginary friend, whom only you could see
and hear, who spoke your special language?

IMAGINE!

When we forget the magic, when we forget to create, how to
play—or determine we're too old, important, or controlled to
stoop to such nonsense—something critically valuable has been
lost. I sensed play's life-giving freedom, energy, and joy while
writing that poem. Play can help us to revive our spontaneity,
open our ears to hear, and therefore help us not to miss our lives!
But oh, what if it were so much more?

Imagination: a gateway to hear the voice of God? You decide
for yourself.

✳ ❈ ✳

*P*lay. *The gateway to change.*

"But, Charlene, what do you mean by *play*? Surely you're
not suggesting I get my old Hot Wheels out of the basement or
drag my doll set down from the attic, are you?" Hey! If that's what
you "heard" me saying (even though I didn't), why not? Think
about all the people making a living by "playing" with dolls, teddy
bears, spaceships, and cartoon characters. Imagination loosed
into NASA, our theaters, and the economy! But not to fear; like

engineers with curiosity, there are other ways to play, more adult ways in keeping with your decorum. [MOMENT OF TRUTH: People of *constant* decorum are highly suspect to me. They often don't seem to smile as much as other folks do either. But I get that decorum is very important to many, so I shall respect it here, even though I have already previously ripped on it. *See* how nice I can play?] A few common forms of adult play that come to mind: golf, bridge, exercise, cooking, riding horses, dancing, stamp art, sudoku, and doing lunch. Of course the list could go on and on. However, what is one person's play might be another's torture. While jogging gets one man jazzed and all aglow, every step is nothing more than an act of pure work and self-discipline to another. While snickering to herself about her winning poker hand is play to Jackie, thinking about all those numbers and calculating the odds is pure agony for Estelle.

The most beautiful experience we can have is the mysterious. It is the fundamental emotion which stands at the cradle of true art and true science . . . I am satisfied with the mystery of the eternity of life.

ALBERT EINSTEIN

I recall the day a friend of mine encouraged me to write a book on the topic of play, since I am so good at playing. "A book for the fun-impaired," is how she put it. Fun-impaired. That's just how she felt about herself. Until . . . the day she called me all breathless and excited. "I *do* play!" she gleefully announced. "I just figured out that dreaming up new marinades for tofu *is* play for me!" [KNEE-JERK MOMENT OF TRUTH: I'm sure I don't even have to say it.] But as we chatted, I realized she was right. She *was* allowing her imagination to run with her creativity until together they cooked up a magical tofu dish. *Blammo, and off the tee she sailed!*

Magical tofu dish. Now, that's either self-explanatory, an oxymoron, or completely inexplicable. [MOMENT OF TRUTH: I love pad thai and I always order it with tofu rather than chicken. It just "goes" better. So perhaps tofu *is* magical and not just a bland combination wad of sponge and mush.]

❖❀❖

In any aspect of our lives in which we desire change, what if we approach it with a spirit of play rather than one more thing we need to work through, gut out, smack off the tee or into shape? (Wa-hoo for pluck-and-play!) Sure, our Magical Express might occasionally derail, but perhaps it just hasn't arrived at the right station yet, the one where laughter helps move us forward again. No matter how serious the quest, if we approach change with a spirit of curiosity, a sense of adventure, and allow our imaginations to lead the way, isn't it possible that the task before us, including our walk of faith, might not be so difficult after all?

❖❀❖

Imagine *this* while you're gearing up to tackle your next project: *You* are Albert Einstein, who believes imagination is more important than knowledge. *You* hold the power to imagine yourself doing great and wondrous things. *You* are capable, creative, a genius who approaches grand cosmic questions about life, time, light, faith, and longing with your resurrected childlike sense of play, where time both stands still and speeds by while you joyfully lose yourself to The Zone.

Hey! You're supposed to be imagining you're Einstein! Do it, please.

Now imagine you are *not* Einstein. (Exactly, Charlene.) Remember that you are *you*, but you borrow from Einstein's greatest asset: the freedom to believe that wonder is good, previous popular assumptions might be incorrect, and by golly, you *can* have the courage to do something new and marvelous. Maybe *you'll* do something that will go down in history as one of the world's greatest discoveries! Go ahead, just give it a try. Just once. For right now. Just see how it goes.

Perhaps you need to begin by reading one of your favorite creative and strangely intriguing books. Maybe a novel on time travel or a tome on archetypes. Maybe you should buy yourself a set of jacks (yes, with the ball and the jacks) and see if you can still "pig over the fence." How might it go for you and one of those new remote cars you ogled at Sharper Image but talked yourself out of? Or perhaps you could buy yourself some glow-in-the-dark stars and stick them up on your bedroom ceiling, arrange them in a smiley face or a new constellation named after you. How about inviting the neighbor kids over, dragging every sheet and blanket you own to your living room, and letting them help you build a fort out of furniture, dish towels, skirts, scarves . . . whatever it takes to resurrect your colorful and playful talents. Then eat a picnic inside your awesome creation and imagine what it would be like to live there when the prairie winds, or the blue moon, or the coyote's howl arrive.

~~~~~~

If we wonder often,

the gift of knowledge will come.

ARAPAHO PROVERB

~~~~~~

Or your spouse.

Go ahead. I double-dog dare you to think outside the box, or at least to allow your inner child to once again come out and play. Just for now. Just this once.

I triple-dog dare you to pick up your Bible and imagine it is a letter to you from a loved one, rather than approaching it as a set of rules and regulations, many of which you don't even understand. Open the cover with the same heartthrobbing exhilaration you felt the first time *he*—that cutie you'd had your eye on for a long while—passed you a note in high school. Hide in the corner and read from the book of John as if you were striving to get a sneak peek (don't want anyone to catch you doing this!) at those wonderful words of love. Imagine there is a Friend dwelling *inside* you who can bring those words to life, who can help you *feel* the love of the author of your faith.

I quadruple-dog dare you.

I ask you.

I implore you to find out what God, who loves you, has to say about his desire for you to live life to the full.

While driving down the same stretch of semicountry road several times a week, I often noticed a gentleman, a stranger to me, walking along the ditch, notebook in hand. His car was sometimes parked nearby; other times he'd journeyed a long way from his wheels. He walked from fence post to fence post, checking something, jotting it down. Finally, one day when I wasn't in a hurry, my curiosity got the best of me so I pulled over. "If you don't mind my asking," I said, speaking to him through my open car window, "what is it you're doing?"

"I monitor the bluebird houses. Would you like to see something amazing? Ever seen a bluebird egg?" he asked, his twinkling eyes revealing his own playful pleasure in his task. At that point in my life, I wasn't sure I'd actually even seen a real bluebird, let alone one of their eggs. I pulled the car off the road, parked, got out, and began to follow him. Atop the fence post perched a little way in front of us was a wooden house. Before we got there, a stunning bluebird landed on its roof, studied us for a moment, and then flew off. *Oh!* The man turned and smiled at me, nodded, then up toward the little house we walked, right into the backdraft left by the bluebird's swooping beauty. The man beckoned me to step right up next to him, then he tilted back the hinged roof to the house—house number twenty-three, my birth date!— and tilted the perfectly round nest my way so I could behold the two blue eggs. *Oh!* It was as if they'd been waiting there for me all along. Waiting for me, with the curiosity and trust of a child, to come *behold*.

The gentleman told me bluebirds will lay five (most typical) or six eggs, only one a day until they are done. He looked at his notebook . . . Yup, number twenty-three had only one egg in there yesterday. Sometimes, he said, they lay white eggs; nobody knows why. Mama will incubate them for seventeen days. Then, more beautiful bluebirds.

He finally closed the tiny roof and we walked back up the hill toward my car. We watched Mama swoop back, land on the house, and stare at us with nothing short of regal posturing. It was as if she knew we'd dropped by simply to admire the precious deposits she was making to this earth on God Almighty's behalf.

✻❃✻

*I*magine what *you* might behold, witness, become a part of, if you weren't afraid to talk to strangers.

Do not be afraid, little flock,

for your Father has chosen gladly to

give you the kingdom.

Luke 12:32 NASB

Imagine how your life might be different if you weren't afraid.

✻❃✻

Worry is a misuse of the imagination," said Mary Crowley. *Imagine* what your life could be like if you believed *that*.

13 * the land of odd

Stop, Crop, and Roll

With our imaginations aglow and a new dream in place, in awe, we leap into a new adventure because we believe the safety net of God's love—maybe even worldly success, and at the very least the Land of Do-overs (or a fishing award, more on this later)—will appear. Wahoo! And then, then we find ourselves in a foreign place. Oh boy. Perhaps it's a new romance that does indeed—*Surprise!*—exhibit possibilities. (But are we ready for a real relationship?) Or we dive through the open Multiple Listing Service window and purchase that new house or condo before someone snags it out from under us. (Buyer's remorse is a real thing, although thankfully it doesn't last forever. Right?) Or say we're finally decided to take that mission trip—but now we learn we need to get some monster vaccinations if we want to commit. (Are we *that* serious?) Or we at long last muster up the courage to register for a poetry-writing class. But . . . *now* we learn they're going to make us *share* what we write! (Why didn't someone explain the rules before I walked into this room full of *everyone* who looks more creative than myself?)

A heat flares within us, as if we've suddenly discovered we've entered the restroom of the wrong gender rather than simply trying something new. Our first instinct is to flee. (And for the record, I agree that we *should* flee the wrong bathroom.) We long to return ourselves to the Land of Boring (the familiar) since we are in way over our heads *here*. We want to go back to where we've previously camped, because we know that at least there, we can maintain the status quo and live to tell about it. Yes, we've teed off and maybe even landed on the green, or we so badly sliced our risk that we've ended up on another *course* offering even *more* potential and possibilities than we could have imagined. Wow! But still . . . it's all so unfamiliar. So scary. We're used to doom and failure. *Now* what? We feel like we've been set adrift on a barge that's barreling down a swiftly flowing river toward—*yikes!*—"SUCCESS" with not even a rudder or tugboat to guide us, or an anchor we can throw overboard to create enough drag to at least slow us down.

We are in over our heads.

We've dreamed a dream, done a tad of research, and taken that step to, at the very least, stretch our comfort zone. But now, whether we've failed or succeeded, how do we survive this new Land of Odd, especially when we find ourselves on the edge of freak-out?

STOP! CROP! and **ROLL!**

STOP! Just *stop* for a moment. I mean S-T-O-P stop. You've probably used up a huge deal of energy igniting this risk and now it's time to recoup some of it. So stop. Sit down. Or stand up for a better view. Whichever you haven't done yet, do it. Look around. Take note of your surroundings. Notice if there are others who look lost, excited, scared, or more knowledgeable, more *seasoned* than yourself at negotiating this new Land of Odd. Talk to your smile until it listens, then smile at those who surround you. Resolve to stay right where you are—at least for a spell. Perhaps you don't yet have enough information to make a fair analysis. Just S-T-O-P and stay put until you do.

CROP any negative inner talk, as in revisit chapter 8 before you become sick of listening to yourself and bail just to shut yourself up—again. Talk *nice* to you. Applaud your courage. You're on a new adventure! Temporarily C-R-O-P your current cast of nonsupportive friends and naysayers. What do they *really* know about your new adventure anyway? Have they been here? Seen this? Done that? Well, not in *your* shoes, they haven't!

ROLL with the punches. Okay, perhaps things aren't going the way you expected. Hey! Maybe that's *good*. Sure, maybe "they" don't do things here the way you've always done them. But then again, *maybe* if you become soft-cornered enough to *roll*, you will learn to roll out some new tricks that will delight your soul, lighten your load, or advance your career. Could be you'll induct yourself into a new way, a better way, to brave not only this new Land of Odd but the rest of your life.

Braver yet, consider this: maybe you're supposed to be here because you've arrived as the *teacher*!

Do not fear the Land of Odd; embrace it. Saddle up and ride it out.

Expect the unexpected.

❖�֍ ❖

Sometimes we learn the most valuable and victorious lessons by watching children navigate the rough waters with nothing more than happy hearts and rudders of persistence. Such was the case at the annual youth fishing derby held during Winona Steamboat Days. Prizes are given for the weightiest fish, the smallest, the most cumulative weight for five sunfish, the prettiest, and the ugliest. At least those are the categories they've always given prizes for *before*. (Did you feel the windup?) Join me now as we step back into my memory portfolio.

❖✖ ❖

After registration, children, their older siblings, parents, and grandparents begin to flank the shores of East Lake Winona near Franklin Street. This is the third year George and I have taken our lawn chairs, picked a shady spot, and watched the busy, oftentimes hilarious action. We sit behind a family consisting of what looks to be three grandparents and one dad fishing with a girl, five years old, and a boy, three. While the grandma positions her lawn chair under a shady tree away from the water, she also stays close enough to observe and occasionally urge one of the menfolk to make their active little boy *back away from the edge of the shore!* It takes all three of those men to keep up with the nonstop baiting, casting, untangling, reeling, and dehooking fishing/catching action of their two pint-size entrants. "I need a break." The one grandpa moans, with still forty of the ninety-minute fishing time remaining. Their three-year-old fisherman can maintain only fits and starts of focus. But that little girl, well, she fishes with determination, perseverance, and a smile. No breaks for her.

I notice something unusual about this family, though: they aren't keeping any of the fish. They are all about catch and release, which is no way to cash in at *this* derby—unless you have a temporary holding bucket (which they don't), or you run your biggest-yet catch over to the announcement stand, have it weighed, then run it back to the water before it stops gasping. Of course it doesn't take long for word to spread regarding the current big-fish weight to beat, so the longer into the contest, the less running we see. A quick eyeball-to-eyeball with each catch lets contestants know if it's worth the trip in this heat.

I decide it's okay if this family doesn't want to compete. (Nice of me, huh?) They'll still get their hot dogs, chips, and soda pop after the fishing stops. But everything changes when the little girl reels in a fish. Although it isn't very big, she announces to her grandpa, who is trying to catch it as it flies through the air at the end of the line attached to her wildly waving pole, "It's so *pretty*!"

I've momentarily stepped up close to the action. Grandpa looks up at me and says, with a condescending smirk and a head shake, "She thinks it's *pretty*."

"Did you know there's a prize for the prettiest fish?" I ask, to which Grandpa pays no attention but to which the little girl shouts, "We *gotta* enter him, Grandpa!"

"You don't want to have to wait around for *that*, do you?" the tired old soldier asks his precious one.

"YES!"

Grandpa shoots me an evil eye (I back away), checks his watch (still thirty minutes remaining until the contest ends), then sets about the business of figuring out what to do with the "pretty" fish. *Right*, the look on his face continues to communicate.

Guess what? They don't end the fishing until twenty minutes later than they said they would, and now they have a chaos of kids dumping the contents of their buckets. Fish flop this way and that, springing up from the earth like they're hot-button-propelled. Humans of all sizes dive around after them trying to determine, then snag, their biggest five for the weigh-in. Those in charge make the announcement that they're going to go ahead and let everyone eat while they finish wrangling around and making decisions, then they'll dispense the prizes. The tired grandpa who gave me the evil eye decides he is not waiting around for all of *that*, and neither is the other grandpa. This leaves Dad, who has tried to dissuade our little blondie (yes, I have claimed her at this point), Grandma, and the little brother, along with the unrelenting fisher girl and her now-dead fish. Those in charge have yet to ask the kids to bring their prettiest and ugliest fishies up for judging, although the little girl and her dad stand right next to the weigh-in booth the entire time, me close behind them. I feel not only invested but *responsible* for Dad's simmering face. After all, if I'd just kept quiet . . .

George and I are sure of one thing: the guy cooking the hot dogs is ready for this event to be over. They only thought to bring one pair of tongs to the grounds, which the Steamboat Days Queen and her court are using to insert the hot dogs (which the cook carries to the steamer in a tray) onto the open buns. This leaves the poor cook turning hot dogs with a pair of scissors and a wet rag.

Nearly forty minutes after the fishing was originally to have ended, they start announcing the prizewinners. While one man reads from the yellow piece of legal paper smeared with fish slime, the other retrieves the prizes from the prize table and hands them out.

But *wait*! They haven't asked the kids to amass their prettiest and ugliest fish yet! Hmm. I step up next to my blondie, her daddy, and her dead fish to interrupt the prize retriever and remind him. He sighs, sidles up to the prize giver, and quietly asks him about those special categories. Now that man sighs louder than even *George* sighs. The announcer mumbles something under his breath to the prize retriever about having the kids do their *own* judging, then letting him know who the winner is. Obviously, these guys have had it.

Oh, like *that* would work. I think. Can you imagine any of the kids not voting for their own? I also notice that no announcement is made over the microphone regarding the self-judging. I think he hopes these last two "events" will go away, and to be honest, I understand. It's hot and it's been a long day. But still, they've *always* had prizes for prettiest and ugliest, and there are kids waiting. I activate by taking it upon myself to start spreading the word.

As said word spreads ("Prettiest fish first!"), throngs of children run to their buckets, once again dumping their fish onto the ground to make their determinations. While they're corralling their beauties and running them over to deposit them (only one entry each) in the leaping circle on the ground, I tell the queen and her court, who happen to be sitting right there, that we need an intervention. "How about beauty judges beauty?" I ask.

The queen tells me she doesn't think any fish are beautiful, but they decide they're game. My little blondie is *so* excited and hopeful to at long last be standing next to her now cloudy-eyed, stiff-as-a-spade entry. All this waiting, and the moment has arrived! You can see it in her eyes: she still thinks her fish is not only remarkable but a guaranteed winner. Her dad is excited, too, since this means they can almost go home. (Grandma and the boy have disappeared to the playground. Apparently one can wait around for only so long to cheer for a dead fish.)

And then the beauty gals make their pronouncement for the prettiest fish, which is not ours. Daddy pats his disappointed blondie's head and says it's time to go. BUT WAIT! Before the kids start to scatter to retrieve their ugliest fish, to everyone's shock, the queen and her court announce that since this group of assembled beautiful fish is already in place, they'll just pick the ugliest from among the same circle. Obviously, the queen and her court want to go home, too.

Without any commiseration, the queen announces that *my girl's fish wins*! She wins a Steamboat Days T-shirt! Dad is happy because he gets to go home. I'm happy because after causing them to wait here all this time, my guilt is assuaged; they didn't hang in there for nothing. But the little girl, well, she isn't sure *what* to be, since before she barely has time to grieve her loss over not having the prettiest fish, her pretty fish just got pronounced the ugliest. How on earth do you emotionally sort *that* out? Talk about a Land of Odd!

"As the worm turns," my dad was fond of saying under peculiar circumstances. Ain't it the truth?

The moral of this story is, um, well, how many do you want to extrapolate? Here's a few that come to my mind.

- You can't win if you don't play. So PLAY. STOP, CROP, ROLL, and STAY. Even if you think the game is over, maybe it ain't.
- Beauty is in the eye of the beholder, as is ugly. Don't let anyone convince you otherwise.
- Two sets of tongs saves burned fingers. (Memo for next year's derby.)
- Perseverance pays off—although not always the way you expect it will.
- Sometimes it takes generations of family members to keep two hooks baited.
- Even the Land of Odd produces *winners*. *See!*

❋

Sometimes (yeah, baby!) you're in a Good Zone, that is, dead-lines met, e-mails caught up on, vacation in front of you. Or kids napping, laundry folded, toenails polished. Maybe you even won the prize you were *after*! You get the drift: all is right with the world. Then, through a series of unexpected events, rather than you diving into the Land of Odd, it creeps up on you. And don't you just know I have another story to share, one that is the perfect example.

❋

My vacation-planning day (Good Zone) turned out to be one of those oddly bad days that actually started the day before. I was eating a salad (yes, miracles do happen) while lunching with a friend. Suddenly I crunched down on something that was not one bit salad-y. Discreetly, my stealth tongue labored to separate the hard, odd-shaped object from the half-chewed lettuce, then maneuver said hard object to the front of my mouth to expel it into my napkin for a look-see. *What in the world?* Upon examina-tion (which I tried to do with, yes, *decorum* so as not to look like I was pawing through stuff I hock-tewied into my hand), it looked to be a piece of tooth. This caused my tongue to further activate a wild search to discover the origin of the deposit. *Aha!* It was the back half of one of my molars, one of the multiple teeth in my mouth composed of more filling than tooth. When I arrived home, I phoned the dentist.

"Emergency! We're leaving on vacation in two days, and half of my molar is missing!"

"Are you in pain?"

"No. But I *could* be. I can just tell. Can you squeeze me in?" Yes, they could. Tomorrow. Which brings us right to the Bad Day I'm talking about. I shall skip the opening details and bring you straight to my sixth shot of Novocain. (Yes, you read that correctly.)

Although I've never had this happen before or since and I wouldn't dream of changing dentists because Dr. Mark is excellent (and makes great pancakes for his sons shaped like little butts—this he tells me when my mouth is full of metal appliances and a record number of wads of cotton), for whatever reasons, the root of this tooth simply won't fall asleep to the Novocain. My tongue, chin, lips, and cheeks are dead to the world, but when he test-drives his drill into the depths of my mishap, YOWZA!

Finally he says, "I apologize. Sometimes these things happen. I think at this point I should just put a temporary filling in there today. It'll tide you over until you get back from your vacation. We can fill it then." To which I respond, "Ah-ing-a-ē-oo-iea." Since all dentists have studied the language of cottonsballsandmetalappliancesinthemouth, he understands me to say, "I think that's a good idea," and we take it from there. Besides, I have a nail appointment (during my acrylics phase) and you don't mess with those, especially not right before vacation.

Since my mouth is dry and yucky, en route from the dentist to the salon I visit McDonald's drive-through. Somehow I manage to get them to understand I want a large diet cola with lots of ice. Now picture this: I'm sitting in the salon chair across from my nail technician, who is working on one hand while I use the fingers on the other to pinch my lips around the straw because my lips cannot feel on their own and I don't want the pop to be pouring out of my mouth as fast as I'm sucking it in. We trade off (next hand for new lip pincher) throughout the procedure until at last my nails are done, which gives me hope that my day is picking up.

Oh, don't I wish.

As I'm walking to my car, I step onto the grass between the sidewalk and the curb at which my car is parallel-parked. I notice the pastor up on a ladder at the church across the street. *What in the world is . . .*

CRASH!

Before I even have time to think, *Oh, I'm falling!,* I am down. My feet are still on the grass but my head and arms have landed in the gutter—the gutter filled with water and muck from recent rains. My right elbow, knee, and shoulder all managed to scrape on the cement and I am knocked silly. I sure hope I haven't broken anything because nobody would see me here, down on the ground between the front bumper of my car and the rear bumper of the car in front of me. After I regain my senses, I slowly start to move. Although my arms are muddy and road-burned, and my pants are scraped clear through at the knee (including through a layer or two of skin), and I'm intensely sore, all body parts seem to move okay. For leverage, I put my hand up on the bumper to heave myself up. That's when I spot the egregious injury: two broken acrylics! Now I am *truly* injured since I've just paid for these! I gimp back into the salon holding my forearm, hand limply hanging down at a forty-five-degree angle, nails out in front of me. My technician is already working on someone else, so I walk up behind the client, hold my hand up behind her, and say, "I haad an assiden. An oo fis me?" Numb tongues do not work well, but I'm just glad it's there. I could have bitten it off and not even known.

She looks from me to her client, as if to indicate "Sometimes people wander in . . ." Yes, she *could* of course repair my damages, but not for ninety minutes. Could I come back? I nod my head.

By the time I get home, I decide to put my waiting time to good use and mend George's favorite pair of black (hang on to your hat) *polyester* (indeed) pants. The seam right under the zipper

that curves down to the bottom of the crotch has popped open—
again—so I get out my sewing machine while grumbling about
how much I hate these shiny pants and how I never want to *ever*
have to sew them again. When I try to thread the needle, I cannot
see the hole in same without my glasses, which I cannot find. I
look everywhere and finally decide I bet I had them on my head
(typical) when I fell down. I determine to look for them when I go
back. But in the meantime . . . for the first time in my aging life, I
have to get out that needle-threader thingie, that giant diamond-
shaped wire apparatus my grandmother used to use—the one that
passes through the needle, then you put the thread through the
giant diamond, and pull it back through the eyehole. By the time
I get George's pants laid out, I've lathered myself into a fit. *How
old am I? So old my teeth fall off in chunks, I can't walk without falling down, and I can't see? And I HATE THESE PANTS!* I mean to tell
you, I sew those babies. I run the racing needle back and forth,
going over and over the seam so as never to have to sew them
again. *Never. More throttle!*

When I remove the shiny polyester pants from the machine,
cut the thread, and hold them up, I discover I've sewn a giant
pucker right at the bottom of the zipper. That black thread is
so buried in the polyester, there is no way—especially without
glasses—to rip it out. So I fold the pants real nice, lay them over
the chair, put my machine away, and head back to the salon.

Yes, I guessed right: I find my glasses right there in the street
where I fell. Where I ran over them with my car when I pulled
away.

That night I phone our sons, which is typical before we head
out on vacation. I can't help but tell Bret every sordid, terrible,
awful rotten thing that happened to me during this Land of Odd
day. I need sympathy. But by the time I'm done, we are both bust-
ing a gut laughing.

"I'm so glad you called, Mom," he says through peals of laughter. "I had a terrible day, too, but yours was worse, and somehow that makes me feel better!"

Magical laughter.

Perspective. Holding those terrible rotten things up to the truly terrible. Sharing them with another, who sometimes says, "You think *that* was something, well, just wait until you hear *this*!"

[MOMENT OF TRUTH: George didn't even notice the wayward pleat in his pants that I hoped would cause him to get rid of them. Now you know why I had to blockade the door to make him notice the SPAM shirt. To this day, the SPAM sweatshirt lives on. Thankfully, the black polyester pants do not.]

❊❈❊

A terrible rotten day. *Another* couple I know gets a divorce. A friend is diagnosed with malignant melanoma.

And yet . . . our neighbor calls and says, "Come see our new baby daughter." Or halfway around the globe, a great-grandmother's crooked fingers gently caress the silky toes of her great-grandson. Venus is so bright that rather than looking like a planet, it appears as if God has poked a hole in the sky enabling all the sparkle of heaven to shine through. "Mom, I got an A!" "Honey, I'm off the night shift." A surprise birthday party. The perfect meat loaf. The spellbinding howl of a coyote. Someone reaches for a hand, pats a back, offers a hug and a prayer.

❊❈❊

D on't allow what isn't truly important to rob you of perspective in the Land of Odd. At the very least, share your stories with someone the best way you know how. If your incident doesn't turn out to be funny, at least you'll have someone to cry with you.

Pretty fish = ugly fish. Sometimes it doesn't matter which wins when you're in it together. If you laugh together, wonderful. If you cry together, may you both cry long enough that you finally come out the other side, where you can laugh again at your sorry, snot-laden self.

Leap. Arrive. Look around. Smile. STOP! CROP! Get ready to ROLL! with whatever. If you give yourself a chance, you might discover that the Land of Odd isn't so add after all. Or that perhaps it's only a mirage and you need to relaunch.

Then again, you might even discover you've at long last arrived in the Land of Plenty.

14 ✻ when it rains, i let it

Responding to Life's Storms

For a long time now, I've tuned in to diversified centurions delivering their best pearls of wisdom as to how to live a long and happy life. Since I'm closer to a hundred than to zero, they've captured my attention. I give more weight to the real oldsters who still speak in coherent sentences rather than buying into everything the Food and Drug Administration (or anything originating with science) tries to dictate to us about aging via the 5 P.M. news. Especially since, for one thing, the FDA people keep changing their minds. Cholesterol is bad. No, good cholesterol is good, and too much bad cholesterol is really bad. Well, as long as total cholesterol numbers don't go over two hundred. NEW PLAN: make that a hundred. And whoops! The pills we gave you for your pain will trash your heart. Oh my! It also seems we need to reverse the food pyramid we drilled into you oldsters when you were youths. And . . . and all the while, none of these scary powerful authoritarians is speaking through hundred-year-old lips. At least not that I've seen.

Before you think I don't respect the folks who work hard to keep us healthy, as you've already read, I owe my life to them. It's just that they don't always get it right, so I listen to those who've survived all the odds, come up with their own philosophy—often contrary to popular opinion—and lived to a hundred anyway.

Some centurions say they never allow a drop of alcohol to pass their lips; others down a martini (or shot of Jack Daniel's or two beers, you get the picture) every night. Some eat right and exercise; others consume a half slab of bacon and eggs 365 days a year and talk about relaxing. Some pray every day and trust God to direct their lives; others claim laughter and kicking up your heels is the key. In an *AARP The Magazine* article, Hank Lang, ninety-four (close enough), thinks his longevity and health stem from the fact that he always keeps birdseed on hand. "The birds and squirrels I feed each day keep me entertained. I have periods of stress just like everyone else, but feeding the animals takes my mind off of it. It's a nice diversion."[1] I laughed when I read this because squirrels definitely divert George's attention, too, but not in a good way. [MOMENT OF TRUTH: George has been known to bang on the windows and yell at the squirrels when they once again figure out how to penetrate the obstacles he's engineered to keep them out of the bird feeder—and he is a manufacturing *engineer*, remember.] Of course I briefly consider all methods (aside from George's) since, hey, these folks lived to be a hundred (or close enough), and they got that coherent-sentences thing going for them, so obviously *something* works. Yes, I'm all ears!

But one day during a television interview, a gentleman who had surpassed one hundred years of age was asked to share *his* secret to longevity. With eyes all a-twinkle (and why would I want to listen to a sourpuss?), he breathed a remarkable Truth into me, one I shall never forget. "When it rains, I let it," he peacefully said. His smile lit up my soul.

❋

There are some things it just doesn't pay to buck against. Why is that so hard to remember? Why do we fret about things over which we have no control?

Or *do* we have control over more than we think?

I mean seriously, might we be able to dink around with literal rain if we take charge of global warming? Should we give the possibility our energies and brainpower? Or is all that global warming talk just a sham spread by a bunch of liberals and tree huggers? (I am not truly asking this question here; I'm just using stereotypical examples from both sides, so please do not e-mail about this. Pretty please.)

Before I make us all insane with indecision, please revisit (yes, *again* with the revisits!) chapter 5, "Always Question Your Assumptions." Educate yourself as best you can, make your choice, and then either activate or decide you simply need to let it rain, whether that be literally or metaphorically speaking. Of course the metaphorical approach is why the "let it rain" man breathed wisdom into *my* soul: I sometimes wear myself out fighting against the unfightable, like the time I tried to walk off a broken leg. Yes, I truly did that until I nearly passed out from the pain. Then I was afraid I *wouldn't* pass out and that the pain alone would kill me. That was the first time I broke my leg.

Then came the second break.

✽❋✽

Time line: End of the first week in January 2007.

Location: The midst of the Christmas-everything mess. The contents of all twelve of our Christmas boxes of ornaments and decorations are disassembled but not yet reboxed. They're strewn in piles around the living and dining room. All of the outside decorations are tossed helter-skelter throughout the garage.

Mental state: Need I say more?

The beginning of my down(kaboom!)fall: Since all the Christmas-everything boxes are still out of the attic, therefore currently not blocking the path just inside the entryway, it comes over Big George that this would be a convenient time to drag everything *else* out of the attic—everything we've been stuffing up there for the past thirty-seven years. And so he does.

He sorts the contents of *those* billions of boxes until they, too, are strewn wall to wall in the garage—surrounding the still-unpacked outdoor Christmas decorations. Imagine the chaotic mess throughout our entire dwelling place! For instance, our youngest son just turned thirty-six, and while packing the fake garland, I'm also discovering a pile of his baby clothes. Or are those mine? While still wading through mounds of jingle bells on the main floor, I discover a stack of giant bones in the garage. *What on earth?*

Don't *tell* me! But yes, it's true: the bones are remnants of our handmade Halloween cannibal costumes. ("No admittance to the party without a costume" the invitation from thirty-seven years ago said.) We visited meat markets and boiled all the meat off those bones, which we wore in our hair, dangling from our waists... "It's a good thing you didn't die and have someone else find those bones in your attic!" our neighbor later says.

[MOMENT OF TRUTH: In actuality, the party turned out to be a surprise postwedding shower and we were the only ones in costume. Everyone else dressed up in their Sunday best, just so we could feel all the more doofus.]

About three days into the height of George's (okay, *our*) mess, I buy plastic storage bins of every shape, color, and size. It's not only time to get rid of stuff, but to trash the stinky, decaying boxes housing some of the "good" stuff (hahahaha! HAHAHAHAHA!) we want to keep. Now picture piles of storage containers adding to the chaos.

For two days, I endlessly sort and pack Christmas stuff back into the better cardboard boxes and into some of my new colorful containers. Packed cartons are now stacked throughout the living and dining room; the attic, with access up through a closet in our upper level, is empty; the garage is disastrous since there is now a giant give-away pile going. I'm on a terror of a determined roll to create complete order and harmony in our home. Another few hours on the Christmas stuff, and I hope to be able to turn my full attention to the garage. I hear the buzzer on the dryer. The last load of Christmas linens (you know the one) is done. Lickety-split, down the basement stairs I go. When I get to the bottom of the steps . . .

CRASH!

As it turns out, I was *not* at the bottom. Unbeknown to me, I had one step to go, one step I took toward the dryer—into thin air. And guess what? No matter how much hot air I can sustain or spew at any given time, it turns out I cannot *walk* on air.

George, who was already in the basement and looking right at me when I crashed [MOMENT OF TRUTH: Because I was looking at him, because I was LOUDLY on his case about something—sigh], came charging (okay, gimping, due to an upcoming knee replacement! OY!) to assist the splatted and crying me. Before he even reached me, I felt a wave of nausea. It was then I knew I'd broken my leg. The only other time I broke anything, it was this same leg about one inch higher up. Yes, I recalled that familiar wave of broken-bone nausea.

But this time I didn't try to walk it off (ah, the learning curve); I stayed down and did something worse: I became angry about it. Within fifteen seconds after going down, the moment I felt like I was going to hurl, I swallowed down the queasiness with a hearty blast of anger. I pounded my fist on the floor and screamed, "I AM SO MAD! I AM SO MAAAAAAAD!" Seriously. I did this through the agony and tears of my pain. I was so mad at myself for so stupidly missing the last step and stupidly doing so before we were supposed to go on a cruise—which we ultimately had to cancel and I knew it in my gut while I was still on the floor—that I continued expressing these bouts of *so angry* for several days.

Until I remembered "When it rains, I let it." And baby, it was raining. The leg was broken. Done deal. Let it go. Let it rain. Let it heal. I needed to conserve my energy because my body needed every ounce of it to repair itself. Plus, I was going to need a certain amount of mobility in order to be able to help my husband through his surgery.

But back to the floor for a moment. Now picture this: the fallen me in the middle of the mess and not one new plastic storage bin large enough to contain me. ("Don't call Channel Seven news," I quip to my neighbor days later. "They'll discover we're living in 'squalor'!") You cannot imagine what it took for Big George and me (no-usable-knee Mr. and broken-leg Mrs.) to get out of the basement. In fact, I encourage you not to picture that. Emergency room. Pain pill. Temporary cast, which they tell me absolutely *not* to put any weight on. They demand I see an orthopedic doc sooner than later, as in tomorrow. "Don't let them put you off."

Now picture this: about ten crutch-driven hobbles out of my

cubicle in the emergency room, I'm so busy trying to remember how to use the crutches and keep my broken leg in the air that I fall down! SPLAT! I crash on the temporary cast, then my knee, then my hip. I pull my groin. One crutch goes one way and one another. Scrubs-laden staff come running from every direction to help me since I cannot get up off the floor. ("Help, I've fallen and I'm too stupid to stay down, so I've fallen again!") After two men lift me off the floor and into a wheelchair they've whisked from somewhere, they want to know if they need to take me back to X-ray for any other body parts. I'm wondering why none of them put me in a wheelchair to get me to the car to begin with, but I keep my trap shut. "I just want to get home," moans me. [MOMENT OF TRUTH: I'm sorry I didn't let them take me back to X-ray because I've had trouble with that knee ever since.]

Fast-forward: I've been living in a lounge chair the past two weeks since the fall. I was told to keep my broken leg higher than my heart for a month, which is quite the contortionist's trick when one is over sixty. Complex fracture, which means several of them, including a good long spiral mess. The good news: the pieces didn't come apart (thank goodness I didn't try to walk it off since I'd probably have mangled it), so no surgery. Bad news: no weight (and boy, I've got some) on it until at least two more weeks, when I go for a re-X-ray, at which time they'll determine if I can have a walking cast. [MOMENT OF TRUTH: You know you're life has run amuck when you consider the possibility of a walking cast exciting.] George, my long-suffering (in so many, *many* ways), gimping hero has cared for me. Our neighbors came over and moved all the Christmas boxes upstairs and out of our way. George moved the attic stuff (now the garage stuff) from here to there so he could get the cars back in the garage before the snow. Many of the new plastic bins are still empty and waiting. The furniture is plastered against the walls (thank you, neighbors) to make room for me and my crutches, which we figure we'll leave in place since it's a head start on George's upcoming postop needs. It simply is what it is until one or both of us gets ambulatory enough to change it. We have had to learn to cope with living in squalor, which I don't believe is a good book title but nonetheless makes me realize I have enough material to write it.

But we made it. The Geek Squad came and Wi-Fied our house so I could work downstairs. Getting up the stairs to my office courted disaster—okay, *another* disaster. Ask me how I know *that*. (No, don't.) I slept on the pull-out bed in the living room couch and rolled around the kitchen in my office chair.

And then we moved on to George's knee-replacement surgery, which came about two days after I got my walking cast. Thank goodness we took no videos of me hobbling around, a second plaster cast in tow, retrieving his walker so he could get out of his chair. We'd be YouTube megahits.

❖ ❖ ❖

The moral(s) and lesson(s) of this story? Throw away any old boiled bones you might be keeping for reasons unknown to any sane human, and do it now. Give thanks for each unhindered step you take. Thank God for your friends and neighbors; we were humbled by the generous gifts of time, resources, and food with which they graced us. Kornflake, our faithful dog, *still* sends out a barking shout to our kind friend Doris, who took him for a daily walk during our healing onslaught of old-age tricks.

Be a good friend and neighbor to those in need. You can't imagine what phone calls, cards, and especially in-person visits meant to us.

And remember, be careful whose case you're on since he or she might be the very person from whom you'll soon receive oodles and oodles of grace. Then after you've filled up with bountiful grace, be prepared to quickly extend it to someone else (such as he who needs a knee replacement) who also needs to learn to let it rain—until the rain stops and life once again moves on.

There is no sense in fighting against the unfightable. When it rains, let it.[1]

❊ ❊ ❊

This would be a good place to S-T-O-P. (You should be getting better at that by now.) We're going to engage in a great exercise here. Trust me, it will be worth it. Go right now and get four pieces of paper and a pencil with a big eraser.

Ready? (I am not fooled; go get them.)

Start by arranging two of the pieces of paper side by side. At the top of one, write THINGS I FIGHT FOR. At the top of the other, THINGS I FIGHT AGAINST. Then start making your lists. Be honest. Then we'll think about the rain.

Sorting hint: perhaps rather than fighting against world poverty—which is too big for any one person to tackle—you could place that into your fight-against column under "homelessness in my area."

Now that you've made your lists (right?) and utilized my great sorting hint, let's start with the "Things I Fight Against" list. Are there items on that list over which you have no control? *Seriously?* Or might you just *feel* powerless because you haven't yet worked your way to the power position, discovered the right knowledge, or found the allies who can effect change? After this *serious* reevaluation, if you found you *did* perhaps list a few items you continuously FIGHT AGAINST that *are* out of your control, figure a way to extract what you might fight FOR about them and move them to your "Fight For" list. If you can't find that kind of positive power in the issue (and I'll offer a bit more defining help in a moment, should you need to go back), get out the third piece of paper, write LET IT RAIN across the top, and move the item there.

Should you need to ignite your *creative, imaginative* evaluating skills, let's look at a few hypothetical "no power" examples and see if there's anything you can or cannot, should, or should not do about them.

The personality of a child. I'm not talking about occasional misbehavior, but the basic introvert or extrovert, stubborn or pliable types of attributes. Of course I'm not suggesting you give up on the child and cross him or her off your list—although isn't that tempting some days? But by trying to find a way to FIGHT FOR the personality (trust me on this if you have a stubborn child; right, Brian?), you can stop trying to change the impossible (FIGHT AGAINST) and move that child onto the FIGHT FOR paper with the goal to fight for channeling that stubborn energy. [MOMENT OF TRUTH: We used to think Brian would be either president of the United States or a roller-derby king. Instead, he's an engineer. It turns out channeled stubbornness makes for good quality control.]

The size of your feet. Why spend energy being mad about things like this? Stop shadowboxing by wearing too-tight shoes to make your feet appear smaller and just let them be big and beautiful—and comfortable. Shop *for* comfort instead of fighting *against* large feet. When you're as old as I am, you'll thank you, honest.

A broken leg. Duh.

Money in the bank. At this moment, it either is or it ain't 'nuff, and if it ain't 'nuff, stop feeling powerless. Consider fighting *for* a plan to dig out. Switching attitudinal gears can give you just the mental boost you need to seek the help you need, such as learning how to consolidate debt, becoming a wiser spender, and learning how to make smarter choices about who or what to pay off first.

Weather. Setting aside the greater global-warming issue, isn't it time we quit giving so much of our energies to the Weather Channel? Yes, be alert to things like hurricanes and tornadoes, but don't spend your every TV-watching hour glued to the Weather Channel, which often sends you to bed angry that tomorrow is the one day you can get out on the golf course, and now *look!* It's going to *rain!*

They are so often flat-out wrong, and of course they are since there is still no human way to stall that giant cold front or blow it on through. We are grateful for their best guesses and helpful warnings, but why waste this glorious evening getting your knickers in a knot yelling at the weatherman when you could instead spend a lovely night visualizing tomorrow's chip-in from the seventh fairway? And maybe you will *make* that chip! (Professional athletes often say there's power in the visualization technique.) Maybe you'll do so as sunlight streams across your back, or maybe it'll happen in a drizzle or you'll have to clear the course due to lightning. Maybe if it's clear weather, you'll four-putt. The thing is, you don't know, but possibilities abound. Just don't give away *this* moment's precious hour fretting over what might be nothing more than a miscalculation about tomorrow—and "rain."

✳ ❉ ✳

The Weather Channel. Oy. Like an old vinyl record, I seem to have a scratch here that is momentarily (please, God!) holding me in a worn groove. George is a Weather Channel guy, as is

Bret, our oldest, who says he likes to watch the big storm prowling across the map of the country and say, out loud, "Look out,
Nebraska!" George, on the other hand, bemoans the fact that it
either is or isn't going to rain or snow, and he always seems to be
rooting for one of those. Or against it.

Check out this MP memory of mine. First thing in the morning,
George says to me, "It might rain tonight." He goes on to explain
that he isn't sure, though, since neither was the Weather Channel when he went to bed last night. While I'm grabbing my keys to
run an errand, he determines he'll bring some stuff in from the
yard sometime today, just in case. I leave, and within a mile of our
house, I have to turn on the windshield wipers. I call George on the
cell phone and tell him he better get moving if he has stuff out in
the yard he doesn't want to get wet, and *now*. His response: "Oh!
I'll go turn on the Weather Channel!"

"George! I'm *out* in the weather one mile from our house and
it's raining!" GADS!

But the surprising fact is, this is *my* bad. I should have filed
George and the Weather Channel under LET IT RAIN and stayed
off my phone. You'd think after all these years I would remember George has to "see" it on TV before he can "let" it. Yes, *I* am
the one fighting a windmill. Watching the Weather Channel is
what he—and millions of others around the world, perhaps even
you—like to do. Maybe watching the Weather Channel is even a
cloaked form of play. Some people *like* to see the swirligigs and
hear the disastrous and triumphant weather stories. They relax
when spending time with their favorite weather broadcasters. I
do recall George and one of his friends speculating as to whether
or not someone had had her baby yet. When I inquired, thinking I'd forgotten about a friend's upcoming grandchild, I learned
they were talking about a Weather Channel broadcaster. They've
grown to care about her like an old friend. Hey, just because

I don't dig the Weather Channel, that doesn't make the likers wrong.

Just let it rain, Charlene. On them. (HAHAHAHA!)

Not nice.

So, in a spirit of maturity and fairness, I've come up with a Weather Channel compromise: if you want, watch it and enjoy it. (As if you need my permission. HA!) But please, just don't let tomorrow's forecast rob you of today's joys. Not if you want to live life to the full.

❊ ❋ ❊

But back to your lists. Take your LET IT RAIN list to the shredder and pray over it before you push it through. Tell God that he's completely in charge of the items listed now because you are moving on since you are powerless over them anyway. If you don't have a shredder, light the list on fire. Unclutch your fingers from any attempts to control the listed details, and feel the relief. Cry if you must, but then gather yourself up and determine that you shall move your salvaged energies—which you will no longer expend on things you cannot change—to your FIGHT FOR list. Which we shall now evaluate. (I heard that sigh.)

Are the things you're fighting for worth it? Really? Might there be someone else who can take up that fight who will be better at it than you? Like an agent (I adore mine), a spouse (sometimes spouses don't get so rattled about the issue, which gives them a clarity to accomplish more), another committee, your congressperson, the neighbor whose issue you've been fighting for but now it's their turn to fight for themselves? If so, grab that fourth piece of paper, write HANDED OVER on it, and move those items right to it. They are no longer yours to handle. Make a phone call or two if you must; hire someone if you can. Do whatever you need to do to hand over things that can be handed over.

Now, what's left on that FIGHT FOR list over which you have power and for which you are the only one who *can* fight this fight—or perhaps determine it's no longer worth fighting for? (Don't forget: sometimes it's time to stop manufacturing your own "cough"; let it go and move on.) If you're *sure* those things still need action, prioritize them. Then consider this: if your first priority for things worth fighing for needs *all* your energy right now, then back-burner the rest of them. Feel the relief in knowing there is absolutely nothing you need to be doing about anything on your FIGHT FOR list other than this One Thing. When that One Thing is finally over, study your back-burnered remains to see if you still care about any of them. Time has a way of reframing things, taking care of issues, dissolving conflict, shifting your perspective.

Time also has a way of raising new issues, more important and crucial than what seemed urgent before.

Fight one worthy fight at a time, and don't forget to take recesses; step back and reevaluate lest you become the irrational maniac who morphs into someone else's main priority on *their* list *they* have to fight against for the sake of *everyone's* sanity. And who needs that?

In all cases, pray over your lists, and ask God to help you use them well.

❖ ❖ ❖

When the real Dorothy, the woman whose spunk, sass, and energy my fictional Dorothy in *Welcome to Partonville* is based upon, became very ill with cancer, toward the end, her waning lung capacity made it difficult for her to speak long sentences. During my last phone conversation with her, even though her voice was extremely weak, her spirit was still strong. She was determined to talk to me. Her message was potent.

"Since I've been ill," she said, the illness not only robbing her breath but knocking her usual hearty voice down to low volume, "I've realized more than ever"—she took a deliberate breath here—"that there are things over which I have no control." Breath. "*Whatever* has become my favorite word." Breath. "You can end just about any sentence with *whatever*." Breath. "See what I mean?"

Yes, my dearest Dorothy, I see. I feel. I read between the lines. I learn.

Whatever.

When it rains, I let it.

Whatever.

Feel the peace, even in the midst of the terrible pain.

❋

*D*ear Lord, thank you for helping me to remember that you are in charge, even when I am lost. I give all my whatevers to you. Amen.

❋

*F*rom the time I was little until my father died, when I would occasionally get to talking negative about someone or something, carrying on longer than just a healthy unloading, my dad would ask me, "Why do you want to be that way?"

"What way?"

"So negative?"

"Well, because *blah, blah, blah, and blah-blah*." *Now* he should get it.

"Yes, but why do you *want* to be that way?"

"Why do I want to *be* this way?"

Then he would remain silent so I would have to think about it.

Why do I want to be this way?

Why *do* I want to be this way?

Why do I want to be *this* way?

The truth is, I *don't* want to ensnare myself in a net of negativity. What I choose to feed is what grows. (Reread that sentence.) Dad's right: I need to stop feeding this bout of *blah-blah-blah* if I don't want to grow into a negative person. I am not normally or naturally a negative person, but sometimes . . . *Stop coughing!*

But there came a time, a time when I was so angry, outraged—*filled* with rage—about something that I could barely see straight. My throat constricted, my blood pressure escalated, and I spat venom. I could not stop feeding the ire of a betrayal—a betrayal someone knowingly perpetrated against my father. I *needed* to be "that way."

❋ ❋ ❋

But, Dad, things aren't the way they appear. Can't you see that person is emotionally blackmailing you, further taking advantage of your giving spirit? Don't you understand he's not being *sincere*—which you've experienced before when the same offender delivered the first great offense, the one where he grabbed hold of your heart, then manipulated it until he even had you monetarily subsidizing the despicable setup?"

"Char," my dad asks, his eyes revealing the wound *I* am now inflicting by trying to get him to dwell on what we both know is true, "why do you want to *be* this way?"

"Because, Dad, *you're* not being 'this way,'" which implies wising up, pulling the plug on the sick relationship, getting even, exposing the self-serving con artist to everyone and anyone who will listen, which my feet of clay suddenly long to do. "You're not holding him responsible, Dad." But mostly, I want to say, *I need to be this way*—and this is what breaks my heart the most—*because you're not protecting yourself from yet* more *hurt*.

"Don't be that way for *me*," he says, knowing exactly what I mean, even though I haven't vocalized the sum total of it. He's heard warnings from me before about this person's character and intentions. But he has decided—because he always does—that he cannot and will not be *any* way that causes him to get stuck in wounds, bitterness, or vengefulness.

He cannot and will not be unmerciful. That is not my dad.

Yes, he knows the truth of the situation, which is why my push for justice reslices and redices the wounds inflicted upon him by the offender, the wounds my dad chooses to cover with mercy and grace, excusing the rip-off by saying things like "Well, he's been through so much." That is an ongoing excuse right out of the wrongdoer's mouth, which said offender continues to use to wheedle yet more of everything from my dad's kindness.

This is what kills me the most: I am one who knowingly—same as the offender—inflicts more wounds. [MOMENT OF TRUTH: In choosing to continue to root myself in "*this* way," *I* am now a perpetrator of a worse nature than the offender: *I* am one who berates the merciful.]

The guy knows my dad cannot, will not, take up arms, and so, yes, he takes *further* advantage. The cheating and monetary gouging escalate until there is nothing left in the well of either my dad's financial or emotional reserves.

All he is left with is unconditional love.

Turn the other cheek. The greatest of these is love.

My dad spent a lifetime giving people second and fortieth chances. It's one of the things I love most about him, this remarkable giving of self and resources, this extending of grace of which *I*, time and again, have been the recipient. It's one of his brightest attributes, another of the remarkable gifts that makes him so dear to me and to so many others.

The very thing that makes him an easy target.

Still, no, if I think long and hard about the father I love, I *don't* want him to be "*this* way," which is not *his* way. Rather it is my wrong way.

But in order for me to change my way, I'll need to lay down my right to be angry. Yes, I'd like to think I have righteous anger, but the truth is, when we continually wound those we love—when we injure the victim—there is nothing righteous about it.

❖ ❀ ❖

Soon after my father's death, when I'm forced to go through his personal belongings, I come across *proof* of the emotional blackmail in the perpetrator's handwriting. These notes to my father are outrageous and evil. I rail out loud. My blood pressure rises again. I want to gouge out the perpetrator's eyes.

Then it hits me anew: I do not honor my father, who died with peace in his heart over the situation, by once *again* insisting on being this way. My rage does nothing to exact revenge on the perpetrator, but it is killing me, robbing me not only of my peace but of my health, since my blood pressure skyrockets when I allow this to own me. (Since my father is gone, there is no sense acting on any of it now anyway—although I tuck the notes away, just in case, with them, I might one day spare someone else the perpetrator's manipulations.) I *must* lay down my anger. Give it over to God. Ask for forgiveness for wounding my dad; give thanks to

God that there was time between my father's terrible manipulation by the offender and his death for *him* to heal, for me to pipe down, and for us to simply love each other the way we did best.

There is not room in me for both this horrible, resurrected dark rage and the consuming crushing grief from the loss of my father. Yet I stick my nose in my Bible and find myself claiming verses where heads are dashed against stones, which I don't think is why they're in there, but which nonetheless give me a brief pocket of hateful relief. I am human. Others in the Bible were human. We get *angry!* But shortly after claiming Old Testament death and destruction for the wicked, the New Testament once again reminds me I'm feeding all the wrong things if I desire God's best design for my life.

To you who are ready for the truth, I say this: Love your enemies. Let them bring out the best in you, not the worst. When someone gives you a hard time, respond with the energies of prayer for that person. Luke 6:27–28 MES.

Love my enemy? In the beginning, it's too much to ask. All I can do is to take a baby step toward trying not to hate him. And the *only* way I find I *can* begin to melt my anger against him is to begin praying—for both of us. I begin praying for forgiveness for wounding my father and that the perpetrator one day turns to God to assuage his guilt, for how could *anyone* live life to the full with such a burden? Yes, I pray for us both.

We *all* need to turn things over. We *all* need to ask for God's forgiveness, and the forgiveness of others.

We all need to *receive* forgiveness, and God never stops dealing it out.

Bless you, Father God. Thank you, Abba.

❖❋❖

"Why do you want to be that way?" I hear my dad gently asking me during a slip-sliding moment long after he is gone from this earth.

I don't. I don't.

Thank you, Dad.

Of course, when Dad was still alive, even when I was wholly "that way," "*this* way," or any other way, he extended the same grace to me as he did to the offender whom I allowed to constrict my throat and raise my blood pressure—the offender for whom I've since learned to pray without gritting my teeth. After more than a decade of these prayers, I can earnestly say that I can finally talk about this entire saga without feeling anything other than tear-shedding gratefulness for the magnificent lesson and relief. (I have shed buckets of tears just writing this.) What I have learned is how to receive and, most importantly, *accept,* forgiveness from my dad *and* my Father God. Both of them, raining grace on me—which has enabled me to forgive myself.

Let it rain . . . grace.

❖❋❖

I lay down my right to be mad, to seek vengeance, to desire to inflict wound for wound.

I am healing. I can breathe again.

In fact, I can remember the exact moment I first felt that relief. I was sitting out in the cold (late fall after my dad's spring death) in a lawn chair, wrapped in a blanket. I'd been praying as I looked out over the valley from a beautiful viewpoint atop a bluff. Subconsciously, I drew a deep breath that filled my lungs to their full expanse and exhaled, all . . . the . . . way. It's something we do all the time. "Wow, that was a big sigh," we'll say to someone. But rage holds a body so tense—so constricted—that try as I might, I had not been able to draw and release a deep, full, cleansing breath because anger had seized me by the throat until that moment. It simply arrived, as though I'd finally awakened and let go of enough junk to feel God breathing his great healing breath into me. God, who was there to hear my borning cry, who roars in the power of his ocean, who held my dearest Dorothy in his arms as she struggled to let go of earthly breath. God, who tenderly says to the raging me, "I am still here, child of mine."

God, who loves the offender as much as he loves me.

And yet I am human. Undoubtedly I will one day need a refresher course. I just hope I get to the laying-it-down part quicker next time.

Oh, if we could only remember what we know. Help me remember this: *Peace I leave with you; my peace I give to you. Live in peace with one another.*

Peace.

When it rains, let it. *Whatever.* Lay down your right to be mad. *Lord, forgive us. Lord, thank you for forgiving us.* All so that we can live life to the full and breathe peacefully again, and again, and again.

✳❋✳

*D*ear Alpha and Omega God, I ask you now to touch the hearts of my readers in places that need healing. May they search deep within themselves and allow their anger, their unforgiveness—their need for forgiveness—to surface in such a palpable way that they might visualize it buried within their clenched fists. Then, God, might they *ask themselves*, Why do I want to be this way, hanging on to anger, neither extending nor accepting your forgiveness?

Please, God, convince them they don't—*and that they don't have to. Help them to let go of "rights" that cage their freedom until their spirits fall open with relief, open enough to accept your love and forgiveness so that they, too, might fully breathe again. Amen.*

15 * be still and know

Centering in I AM

We are more than physical beings. We are more than father, mother, sister, brother, worker, son, daughter, friend. We are children of God. During our worst moments—when we are at the end of our resources, the end of *ourselves*—clinging to the knowledge that we are indeed children of a loving God is our only hope. "God, it's up to you now." In our best moments, gratefulness dances in our hearts. It swirls and wells within us, energizing beyond our capability to contain it, and so in a great overspill of joy we worship. "THANK YOU!" we shout to the heavens or whisper into our palms as we weep.

Whether we're lost in the busyness, desperateness, or joy of our lives, we need to make room for stillness—the stillness God speaks of when he says, "Be still and know that I AM God"—so we can hear the voice that reminds us whose we are. If we can do that, whether grieving or celebrating, then we will be ready to fling ourselves with abandon into the soft welcoming bosom of God and cling to his love.

It's just that sometimes we don't understand the roundness of stillness. We beat ourselves up for being too fidgety, too scatter-brained, too undisciplined to maintain a quiet time, which some religious folks bandy about as if it were the *only* way to receive a word from God, aside from "being *in* the *Word*," of course. (See their eyebrows pinch together while giving you that "And you *are*"—slight pause—"*in* the Word every day, *aren't you?*")

The Word. Sometimes we just don't get it. We tried it and . . . no compute. More proof that we're not holy enough to *really* be God's children. We think, *Those folks in the Bible study I don't attend because I don't know my Bible well enough know so much about religious rules. They must, because they're always reminding me which ones I'm breaking.*

Frankly, it's all too intimidating. We decide we need to find our own way. So we carve out a time to pray, to get us some of that there quiet time.

Dear God, I want to tell you how much . . . What time is Jessie's doctor appointment today? I'll have to leave here at . . . Wait, I'm supposed to be praying . . . *Lord, please forgive my jitterbug brain. Try as I might to* . . . Hangnails make me nuts. I cannot concentrate until I find the clippers and get rid of this little tag of skin . . . Whew. Got that taken care of. *Dear God, I am a wretch of a person who can't concentrate through* . . . ring, ring . . . *I'm going to let it ring, God, that is if you're even still there. But I guess you are since someone once said you're omniscient, whatever that means.* I meant to look it up. I think it means all-knowing . . . But where was I? Oh. *Dear God* . . . ring, ring . . . What if it's one of the kids?

And away we go.

✽❋✽

We are not worthy. We'll never get in touch with God. But moreover, we fret that neither will God be able to break through our tormented yackety scatterbrains. We're not spiritually mature enough for God to *really* love us. We're sure of it. We need to pick up four more books on prayer and make bigger sacrifices because we're selfish to boot. And to be honest, we're not sure about that whole "Holy Spirit" thing either.

If we could just be *still,* maybe we'd get it.

That's it, I'll take a class on prayer and meditation!

Scratch that one. I don't have time. Surely there's another way. I mean if God really wants or needs to get my attention, isn't he able to accomplish that in a myriad of ways—especially if he's all omniscient like—not just when and/or if I can ever get still enough?

Hmm.

Let me share a few true stories here out of my MP, and you decide for yourself.

✽❋✽

I arrive at church an hour early this morning to seek stillness, to sit in the prayer-worn pew and meditate, look up the Scripture readings in the bulletin ahead of time so I can take them in at my own pace, read what comes before and after in order to settle them into my own context before they arrive in today's message.

I also want to read and contemplate all the lyrics to today's hymns so I don't miss them while I'm striving to make my voice ride all the notes in the appropriate sequence. (Sometimes, at the end of singing a hymn, I wonder if I ever really paid attention to the message within it. But sometimes, even if I don't think about the words, a grab-your-gut musical transition drops my soul to its knees with adoration and worship for my Almighty God. Yes, there's always something about the music.) As I sit in the quiet of the cool stained-glass haven, I decide I'll start with the hymns.

I grab the hymnal and notice a request-for-prayer card tucked inside. There's writing on it. Someone must have forgotten to turn it in when the basket was passed. If I read it, I'll feel kinda like I'm spying, but I decide I'll pray for them now while my heart is open. Before examining the request (I've dropped a few of my own desperate pleas into prayer baskets), I close my eyes and shoot a quick request up to God that I prayerfully cover the re-quester's bases. My preprayer prayer sounds like this: *Lord, help me honor the person who wrote it.* [MOMENT OF TRUTH: A sense of "oh, what a great thing I'm going to do" envelops me, a *prideful* sense of "I am so holy," and I hate it when that sometimes hap-pens. Even more, I hate to admit it, but there you have it.] None-theless, I get ready to pray, because, pride aside, prayer is *prayer.* I turn the card over and read it.

"DAD IS MENTAL," a child's uneven all-caps scrawl declares.

I laugh out loud. My thunderous guffawing reverberates around the empty sanctuary. Certainly a parent striving to keep his or her child quiet (but why do I assume it's a boy?) during the sermon handed him a prayer card and pencil with which to en-tertain himself.

But then I think, *What if dad is mental?*—as in a clinical-mental-illness kind of way? Schizophrenia runs in my family; I am suddenly—and once again—grateful my sons dodged the ge-netic bullet. All pride left behind, I pray, *Thank you, God! Protect my granddaughters, Father. And God,* help *this child and this child's family,* whatever *their needs.*

When I'm done with my heartfelt rendering, a new thought

whisks through my mind, and again I burst out laughing: I wonder if the pastor's rascally son wrote this note and planted it there while thinking, *This will teach Dad to use me in one more of his sermon illustrations!*

Laughter. Silence. Unspoken words. Fleeting thoughts. Pleas. Prideful holiness. Thank-yous. Needs. Hidden messages or face-value funnies. Each a form of communication.

Lord, I give You all of it as I sit here in this sanctuary filled with the Real Me.

Earlier this morning I piled several days' worth of accumulated dishes into the sink (no electric dishwasher here at The Farm) and filled it with soapy water. I birthed the top bowl out of the warm frothy cocoon and started to wash it, but the stubborn dried-on gook wouldn't budge. I reached for the scrubber, then the thought hit me, *Let it soak, Charlene.* Fifteen minutes later, no scrubbing; the gook simply melted away.

This is how God and silence can work on our souls, our worries, our smarminess, the things we think we need to scrub from ourselves. Stop striving. Just park yourself in the giant, warm, divine dish tub of God's protective cocooning hands and be as still as you can until all your gook soaks loose. Then allow the endless supply of living waters to rinse you whole again.

* ❊ *

Where did that beautiful analogy between warm, soak-ing dishwater and God's cleansing hands come from? [MOMENT OF TRUTH: I uttered "WOW!" when it popped into my brain.]

I believe God is always nudging us, breathing thoughtful, help-ful, soothing words and images of love into our awareness. When we, even for the briefest of moments, tune in, when we take time to STOP (Be Still) and think about the origin of such stunning and rich revelations, we glean a tad of insight into the commu-nicating genius of the Almighty. No sirree, we ain't got nothin' on God!

* ❊ *

One day a friend calls and says, "Wanna do lunch? I've learned something fabulous and I just have to share it. It's life trans-forming!" See me grabbing my keys before she even hears my hang-up click.

We chat, order, eat some of our food. The usual. Then I re-member she has a fabulous thing to share and she hasn't yet done so. Fork parked midair, I ask, "So, what's this new thing you learned? I'm ready to take it in." Chomp-chomp.

Her face brightens just remembering whatever it is. She snaps to attention, leans across the table closer to me, reeling me toward her with this gesture. Then she speaks. "Never . . . hurry."

I wait for the good part but nothing comes. "And?" I say, taking a quick look at my wristwatch.

"That's *it*! Never . . . hurry," she says slower than sludge oozing uphill. "It's like magic or something." She goes on to say how once you determine that you shall henceforth *never . . . hurry*, your stress level goes down. The magical part? Everything still seems to get done on time.

I consider this as we discuss. I think about one of the gauges that declares I am hurrying: bruises. Bruises from hip-checking drawers out of my way. Bruises from running into things because I'm going too fast not to run into them.

We converse about the time we waste on do-overs when, while rushing around, we've spilled or forgotten something. Or missed our turnoff because we were going too fast to make the exit. Minutes lost repeating things because we talk too fast. And yet . . . I'm not convinced. Nice in theory, but nothing magical or practical, I'm sure. Well, at least I got lunch out of it.

Before we part, she says, "I can see you're not convinced." Right. "Trust me!" she implores. "We've spent enough time talking about it now that when you most need to remember it, the words will pop into your head, just like they did after someone told me." Right. I head home to get back to work—running behind with a deadline—and the entire theory vanishes. Type-type-type.

Several days later, I'm taking a shower. Splash-splash the water. Pump-pump the soap. Scrub-scrub the body. And then I hear it in my head. *Never . . . hurry*. But I *have* to hurry since I'm running behind! (Big surprise.) It's like I'm arguing with the concept—dare I say the voice?—in my head. And yet . . . I cannot stop thinking about these words, which seem to have suddenly yawned themselves awake inside me. I decide to slow down, at least a little, since I realize I'm speed-showering. I back up until I'm directly under the strongest force of the shower's pulsating warm river and think about how wonderful the water feels pelting the crown of my head, running down my back, how blessed we are to have hot running water at the turn of a spigot.

I stand there, eyes closed. My mind wanders back to my grandparents' first farm. As the mysterious stuff in a Lava Lamp s-l-o-w-l-y rises and takes its own shape, so, too, details long ago locked in my memory portfolio begin to rise and unfold.

❋ *

I remember Grandma collecting rain in a rain barrel when storms were afoot or pumping water through the kitchen-sink pump. I see her shuttling the water into two giant kettles, which she then heats to wash and rinse my hair . . .

I'm standing head down in the kitchen sink while Grandma's strong fingers run back and forth from my crown to my temples, and again, crown to temples, then down to the hairline of my bangs, around my ears, then gentling into little circles down the nape of my neck. One continuous, relaxing flow. Next, my red-headed grandmother pours the hard-earned warm water over my head as if conducting a great baptism of intergenerational bonding. I hear the suds popping near my ear before she rinses them away. She pats my head with a towel and combs my long, fine, dark locks. Adeptly, she creates a perfectly matched set of secure braids with my squeaky-clean hair. In the aftermath of this ritual, I feel whole, pulled together, loved.

❋ *

When I step forward in the shower and open my eyes, I feel as if I've awakened from a wonderful sleep. *Thank you, Grandma. Thank you, God, for the memory.*

My blurry vision locks on the many bottles of fragrant hair and body products lining the shelf that rims our shower stall.

I've spent countless hours in specialty shops sniffing bottle after bottle until settling on the perfect sensory matches for an array of moods. What a shame, I think, that I'm always in such a hurry, that I've barely taken notice of the scents since I brought them home. I resquirt my fluffy netting thingie with a short stream from the blue one (can't read it without my glasses), lather it up good, lift it to my nose, and inhale a fragrance reminiscent of a fresh rain. Having just bathed in the warm memories of my grandmother's old farm, now I know why this appealed to me. With unhurried intention, I run the foamy softness and calming essence over my body. Again, I rinse. I smile at my double-worshed, as my grandma pronounced it, self. After I step out of the shower, I take my time and actually *dry between my toes*! I feel quiet, peaceful, cleansed.

YIKES! WHAT TIME IS IT? I put on my glasses and check my wristwatch.

It *is* magic, I think. I still have plenty of time! What happened there? Was I going faster than I thought? Did I misread the hands on my watch when I stepped into the shower?

Have I time-traveled?

✸ ❧ ✸

That was the first of many instances in which the magical *never . . . hurry* theory—God-breathed through the mouth of a friend—proved to be correct. I don't get it; I just know it works—unless you're running for an airplane. And then you better make those feet fly. But aside from that, life in the calm lane is a definite enhancement.

Never . . . hurry, and for goodness' sake, don't fret about not hurrying! This, of course, will take some practice. When you least expect it—and likely when you most need to hear them—those two precious words might spring to life in your mind. I'm praying so as I type.

CXFDX43CX [*sic*]

I just took a short break to slice an apple into a bowl and bring it to my desk. When I returned (and I am not exaggerating an ounce of this), the above sequence of letters and numbers appeared—exactly where's it's double-tabbed—along with wet-dog slobbers on my keyboard and a wagging-tailed Kornflake, who looked very pleased with himself. Apparently he felt compelled to continue praying for you in my absence. Although I have no idea what the dog prayer consisting of "tab, tab, CXFDX43CX" means, Kornflake had to not only tab twice but capitalize and uncap to pull this off. Seriously, I have no idea how he did this, but after I made room on my desk for the bowl of apple and have seated myself, he immediately lay down at my feet and dozed off, so it must have been exhausting.

Hey, who am I to think Kornflake's message wasn't God-inspired? After all, he did receive a wonderful blessing this year during the annual ritual pet blessing held outdoors in Homer, Minnesota, at Homer's First United Methodist Church. Pastor Christine blessed him herself!

❋❋❋

While sifting through my basket of DMYL materials, I come across a yellowed piece of newspaper. It's an obituary for my long-ago, long-standing Electrolux man. Not only did he sell me two terrific machines, for years he faithfully kept my sweeper running and supplied me with accessories and vacuum bags. But, I am just realizing, he was the first person, without actually saying it, to encourage me to *never . . . hurry*. Perhaps it's why I've kept a remnant and reminder of his life for all of these years. From the first time he sold me a vacuum, and a few instances in between when he tested my machine, he moved it across the carpet s-l-o-w-l-y, saying, "The biggest problem with vacuums today doesn't exist in the appliance, but the ones running them too quickly over the carpet. I don't know why everyone's in such a hurry today. The machine doesn't have time to do its job." All the while he was talking, he s-l-o-w-l-y moved the beater bar forward a yard, then slowly back over the same strip of carpet.

You know, as with most things, there's a lot of layers to that philosophy. What appliance, tactic, or person might you think needs to be replaced for lack of proper function, when the reality is, you've never given it or him or her the proper time and attention to demonstrate their value because you're always in such a *hurry*?

✿ ✿ ✿

My first freelance writing job happened by accident, sort of. Someone in the Bible study I was attending thought I said I was an unemployed writer looking for work rather than someone who once took a writing class. (God, the purposeful mistranslater, eh?) So when she saw the advertisement for a community columnist, she ripped it out and brought it to our study group the next week. I was too dumb to know I wasn't qualified and therefore had no business applying, but I got the job anyway. (I leaped and the net appeared!) Turns out I could tell a story, even if it wasn't about me. Several months into coping with ongoing deadlines, I started writing feature stories, too.

Within a couple years, an opportunity opened to submit something (again, freelance basis) to a much larger paper, which I did. The teensy tidbit was accepted and ran in a Sunday edition. Shortly thereafter—and much to my surprise and shock—I was told by the smaller paper that if I were to continue publishing in the larger paper, I'd have to give up my weekly column. Although there were no legal legs for this ultimatum, I respected the stand, which was unquestionably a firm one. To sweeten the pot, one of the Big Kahunas at the smaller paper offered me an editorial position. Oh, my stars!

On the one hand, I had a sure offer for advancement working with people I'd come to know and enjoy. On the other hand, the bigger hand (?), I had no guarantee of anything. At that moment, I didn't know if the bigger paper would ever accept another of my ideas, which, in fact, were missing. And yet I understood I was at a risky crossroads (bet you been there!): was I potentially moving from hobby to quasi career here?

I talked to George about it, to my closest friends, and to God. Nonstop I prattled on, making myself and everyone nuts with my indecision. In the meantime, the clock was ticking on the editorial offer; the position needed to be filled.

Then one day a friend, who'd recently moved a couple hours from our neighborhood, phoned and invited me to come see her new digs. Of course my response was to immediately wear her out sharing the details I'd lined out on my now pages-long pros- and-cons lists.

"There's a small river nearby," she said, striving to end my telephonic diatribe. "We can take the tractor inner tubes down there and just float and discuss. Or maybe you just need to float and be quiet awhile." Not until she unloaded the word *quiet* did it hit me like thunder: I'd barely done an ounce of listening. When people gave me their feedback, I was presenting the other side of the coin nearly before they were done with their sentences. "Yeah, but . . ."

In particular, though, I had done no listening for the voice of God, which didn't necessarily mean I'd done no praying. It just meant I'd invested no time in listening for answers.

"I'm coming tomorrow," I said, right after I worked out a few details with George. Yes, we would float, chat, and then I would listen. I would listen to her, and then for God.

The entire drive down there, again and again I reviewed the details of the decision so I could succinctly present them to her. The minute the water swept us downstream, I unfolded those details in a manner that definitely covered the bases. She, playing a bit of devil's advocate—which I usually like to do myself when someone needs to think something through, which is why I like her so much—raised yet more flags for every one of my flags. But spending time with her again made me realize how much I'd missed her keen mind. We decided to use up the last portion of the float each lost in our own thoughts and decisions while continuing to delight in each other's silent presence and the beauty of the passing scenery.

And then the float was over. No matter how hard I'd tried to glaze over and let the sun glaring off the water blind me to my own thoughts, I never shut up in my head, and God never interrupted. Even though I'd spent time visiting, floating, and supposedly relaxing, when all was said and done, I was more keyed up than ever. This was a disaster: tomorrow I needed to give the kahuna my answer—the one I didn't have.

On the drive home, I tried to relax by opening the car windows and blasting the radio. Maybe if I distracted my brain by singing along, it could subconsciously percolate its own conclusion. That's the way Dad used to do it, right? But all I succeeded in accomplishing was to further frustrate myself. The loud music was making my tense self nuts. I turned off the radio and drove along in silence, watching the flat Illinois farmland morph back into the edges of jagged urban development.

Then I began talking out loud to God, or, to be honest, giving God a good what-for. "You *know* I have to make this decision and I *can't*! I tried listening and you didn't talk, so *now* what?"

Stick with me, kid, and don't throw out the anchor.

I heard God's voice in my head as clear as a bell. I can't tell you a thing about the tone of it; the words were just there, and they weren't mine. (If they weren't God's, whose were they? And no, I don't suffer from schizophrenia.) Had there been a *thee* or *thou* in the sentence, I know I wouldn't have listened. I'd have figured Charlton Heston, not God, was talking to me. But this language, well, this was simple, everyday language spoken to the real me. My mom often used to call me kid or kiddo, so *kid* was already a warm, familiar parental term of endearment.

"*Kid?* Stick with me, *kid*? What the heck is that supposed to mean?" Honest, I said this out loud as if I were Bruce Almighty[1] talking to a God only he could see but whom only I heard. I was also slightly offended. I mean, this was an important decision, potentially a career decision, and God's attitude seemed kind of casual if not downright flip to me.

No response. Silence. I repeated the question a few times, then began rolling the answer around in my thoughts.

Kid. *I'd love to be a kid again since all this grown-up stuff is tormenting. Fine.* I'll just be God's kid for a moment and see how that goes.

Of course I *loved* being God's kid. The thought made me smile, which felt very good. I simply drove along in that for a while. "I am God's kid," I repeated. It was so satisfying.

Then, for lack of a clearer or more honest explanation, I knew that the message had been delivered in its entirety. Now it was my task to interpret it. God trusted me to "get" it, which is another way I know it's God's thought and not mine: I blather.

"Anchor." I drove along meditating upon the word, repeating it like a mantra. "Anchor."

Then it hit me that the only opportunity that could be considered an anchor (editorial means real job) was with the people I knew, and just like that, my decision was made. When I awoke the next morning, I still felt sure about my decision, even though I understood I was taking a huge risk since I might end up with nothing. I thanked the kahuna at the smaller paper, the starter of my career (which I hadn't seen coming) for the editorial offer, handed in my resignation, and, through many tears, wrote my farewell column. Before it even ran, the editor at the larger newspaper, the *Chicago Tribune*, contacted me with a story assignment. I went on to write more than a hundred pieces for the *Tribune* before switching nearly full-time to books. (Remember the straw-up-my-nose guy who started *that*?)

Sometimes when we're praying, all we do is talk and talk and talk and then we say amen. Sometimes when we have a difficult decision to make, we gather opinions and feedback from everyone we know, but we forget to consult God first. Sometimes when we listen, we hear nothing.

No matter, sometimes we just need to be as still as we can and listen for the voice of God. We need to trust that God speaks our language, which, whether booming or whispering, is always his language of love.

SOMETHING TO PRACTICE: Have you ever questioned whether or not God still speaks today? Try asking him and then listen. There have been times when the voice of God has arrived in my thoughts, out of the mouth of a friend (*never . . . hurry*), in the words of a hymn, or in the soul-igniting trill of a red-winged blackbird. If you are awake to your life, you'll be much more able to hear.

✻ ❇ ✻

During an intimate and vulnerable sharing time at a women's retreat, one woman got up and told an amazing story. She'd gone through a rough time in her life and, as a result, decided to go looking for God—a God she could finally believe in. She picked up a Bible, but the domineering patriarchal language, as she put it, caused her to set it right back down. She'd been abused by the men in her life. The idea of God as anything resembling a father—especially *her* father or uncle or cousin— was not palatable. (I've heard time and again how difficult it is to imagine a *loving* Father God by those who've been abused.) She started visiting churches in search of God, but God was nowhere to be found. No matter how sterling the sermon, lively the pastor, or friendly the congregation, it all added up to imperfect people, not God. There were always people who ultimately bickered, used unfamiliar religious jargon, or wanted her to get way more personal with her feelings than she deemed appropriate for a group of strangers. Not for the first time in her life, she concluded that God didn't likely exist, so she quit actively looking. Still, she kept her ears open, just in case God decided to speak to her. But, she admitted, in all honesty, she'd pretty much given up.

For the earth will be filled

With the knowledge of the glory of the LORD,

As the waters cover the sea.

HABAKKUK 2:14 NASB

Years later, she fulfilled a longtime dream by embarking on a whale-watching expedition. After a long boat ride of watching and searching for the whales—and like her failed quest to find God, she was about ready to give up the search—a great whale, not that far from her stance along the rail, rolled up out of the ocean. By the time she began to describe the moment when the whale's tail sank back down into the water, she was weeping through the words, " . . . and just like that, there God was. I don't know how else to explain it, but the minute I saw that whale, I knew God existed."

But now ask the beasts,

and let them teach you;

And the birds of the heavens,

and let them tell you.

Or speak to the earth, and let it teach you;

And let the fish of the sea declare it to you.

Who among all these does not know That the

hand of the LORD has done this,

In Whose hand is the life of every living thing,

And the breath of all mankind?

JOB 12:7–11 NASB

She said that God chose to reveal God's self to her through the most unlikely and surprising means: without uttering a single word.

God knows *your* language, too. Listen. With eyes wide open, prepare to hear.

❋❋❋

When, shortly thereafter, our God-seeking, whale-watching storyteller (Thank you to everyone who dares to share their hope-filled stories!) returned to church, everything felt different: she belonged, and God was. She was most comfortable getting to know God first as a beloved mother. Then she came to intimately learn the love of Jesus Christ and the nudges of the Holy Spirit.

And God created man in His own image, in the image of God He created him; male and female He created them. Genesis 1:27. Sometimes we don't think about the breadth of the "in the image of God . . . male and female" long enough.)

＊❈＊

Be still and know that I AM God. Be still enough to listen, even if your leg is jiggling, you're driving fifty miles per hour, or you're talking to yourself, because maybe, just maybe, it isn't you talking after all. Be still enough to consider the wonders of nature, whether they're rising up out of the ocean, sprouting flowers as big as muskmelons, or gulping in your fish tank. Be still enough to pray for yourself and others knowing that God is listening, perhaps dreaming up the most astounding way to answer.

But also keep an eye on your pet. I'm thinking they're up to something when they start praying in typed code. If all our pets start praying together, *look out!* And if they're praying for their own wants and needs instead of ours, it might just start raining catnip, dog bones, carrots, birdseed, or all of the above. Honestly, this notion makes me rethink the root of God's motivation in Exodus 8:1–2 when the Lord said to Moses, "Go to Pharoah and say to him, 'Thus says the Lord, "Let My people go, that they may serve Me. But if you refuse to let them go, behold, I will smite your whole territory with frogs." ' "

Do you think the lizards might have been talking to God about a food shortage, because shortly thereafter, sure enough, a serious—very serious—"smiting by frogs" began.

I'm just kidding. Right?

16 ✻ be a reed

The Breath of God Blows Through Us . . .

In a wonderful little book called *Jacob the Baker* by Noah ben-Shea,[1] there is a line of description about the main character that perhaps expresses an ultimate goal about living life to the full. "Jacob was a reed, and the breath of God blew through Jacob, made music of him." Can *you imagine (yes!)* a more powerful *aliveness* than experiencing the very breath of *God* blowing through *you*? Making *music* of your *life*?

Then the Lord God formed man of dust from the ground, and breathed into his nostrils the breath of life; and man became a living being.

Genesis 2:7 NASB

Power, mercy, peace, patience, forgiveness, unbridled joy, stories beyond measure . . . each set to the perfect melody and rhythm by the breath of God. *Oh*, to imagine God using *you* as one of his melodious forms of communication! To know you've contributed your part to a great crescendo of music powerful enough to transform the world.

OH!

It takes a great puff of breath to release the word *oh!* A great puff of breath that first had to be drawn—but before that, given.

* ❋ *

Jacob was a reed," benShea wrote. If you're a professional musician, you likely already know this, but in case you're not and you don't, there are reeds in more instruments than you might think, including the oboe, bassoon, English horn, and clarinet. But wait, there's more! Did you know there's a reed or two (or more) in each note of the harmonica, bagpipe, organ pipes, and diatonic button accordion?

The wind blows where it wishes and you

hear the sound of it, but do not know where it

comes from and where it is going;

so is everyone who is born of the Spirit.

JOHN 3:8 NASB

But here's the most exciting part: the pitch pipe—the tiny instrument that lets everyone know if they're in tune or not—is a reed instrument. This means that even the instrument making sure we're playing beautiful music rather than a bunch of sour notes needs to have breath blowing through it. Imagine *this:* God's very breath sounding the perfect pitch for your life. *Oh!* Throughout time, reeds have been crafted from cane, wood, plastic, and metal. With all that variety in instrument and reed, imagine the diversity of possible sounds and impactful combinations we could make if we were playing together! From soul-moving symphonies to hard-rockin' measures, moody jazz to country kick, bluesy blues to rollin' reggae—each message within the music would be specially arranged to speak to its recipient, and *you* a *part* of it.

Take a good look around you the next time you're in a crowded place. Think about the mixture of healing harmonies we might create together were we each allowing the breath of God to blow through us. I bet we could not only blow the doors off the Rock and Roll Hall of Fame but break through the shackles of hate.

❈ ❈ ❈

I sang tenor in the high school choir. Whether we were rehears-
ing or performing, I loved knowing my voice played a small
part of the whole reverberation. Sometimes we sounded terrible
that first pass-through, but the more we practiced together, the
better we got. My favorite high-school-choir event took place
miles from my alma mater. We rode a bus to a college gymnasium and gathered with dozens of other high school choirs from
throughout the region. We'd all practiced the same songs. When
the downbeat came and that first magnificent harmonizing sound
swirled and vibrated and reverberated among us, pausing, then
swelling as we followed the conductor's lead, my goose bumps
danced right along. I've experienced the same sensation when
participating in a do-it-yourself *Messiah* in Edmond Chapel at
Wheaton College. Wowie! The more voices, the more magnificent
the impact.

Imagine God making music using *all* of us.

A pastor at one of the churches I attend said, "God's favorite
word is *one*." One people. One God. One big *Hal-le-lu-ia, Hal-le-
lu-ia,/Hal-le-luia, Hal-le-luia,/Hal-lee-ee-lu-ia!*

❈ ❈ ❈

B ut first, we have to be a reed—available, surrendered—and
allow the breath of God to blow through us individually. This
takes courage, since what if our note is nothing more than a pip-
squeak? (Back to negative inner talk and self-doubt again, eh?)

Not to worry. In the beginning (that beginning) 'twas the Spirit
of God that first moved over the surface of the waters to sepa-

rate light from darkness, heaven from earth from sky. 'Tis God who breathes life into us and serves as the great pitch pipe of the world and our individuality, which means our unique song will be perfectly tuned for the recipient's ears *and* our own pleasure. God doesn't play bad music. And even if we did sound a bit on the questionable side, hey, if God can turn water into wine, I'm sure through the Holy Spirit he can turn the cacophony of our heart-string into a symphony. With a wave from God's music-making wand, even our smallest little tunes can fill a slot in someone's top-ten billboard of extraordinary experiences. I know, because on many occasions in my life—many you've now read about—I've been the blessed recipient.

❀✿❀

I first got to know the real Dorothy via e-mail. One day, her son phoned with one of those surprise "voice out of your past" calls—thirty years out of my past. He was passing through town, so we decided to meet for breakfast. That's when he heard me mention e-mail. "My mom refers to herself as the fastest old lady in our town," he said. "She's on her fourth computer-modem upgrade." He told me she e-mailed people of all ages and that their locations spanned the country. At the end of our breakfast, he scribbled her e-mail address on a piece of paper. I tucked it in my handbag and we went our separate ways.

At first I couldn't imagine following through. But since I have grown sons who live far away, on my drive home from our breakfast, I reconsidered. After all, I'd love to receive a message from someone I didn't know saying, "Hi! I saw your baby today and he looked fine!" That's pretty much what I e-mailed Dorothy when I got back to the house. *Blammo!* Even back in the days when dial-up was our only choice, she must have stayed online for hours at a time, since the next time I dialed up, there was her return message. She indicated that somewhere back in the distant past, we'd been introduced. I didn't remember this or anything about her. But her keen sense of humor made me laugh out loud, so I sent another missive. Before long, we were e-mailing each other every day, sometimes many times a day.

She delighted in referring to me as Charlie Brown, a nickname also out of my past—one her son told her about after he and I had met up for breakfast that morning. She continued to brighten my spirits. As we got to know each other better, she began to pray for my road trips and wasn't shy about calling me up short when I needed it. [MOMENT OF TRUTH: I'm sure you'll find this shocking (Ha!—which also takes a great puff of breath to emit), but I can tend to get irritable if not downright cranky when things don't go my way, even in an e-mail.] We became fast and intimate friends. About a year and hundreds of e-mails into our friendship, I knew I needed to meet this older woman. She was the first person to fill a gaping mentoring hole in my life since the death of my mom.

At the end of my five-hour road trip, there she was standing on her front porch waiting for me. We threw our arms around each other as if we'd known each other forever, which is exactly how it felt. She showed me around her charming house, then we had a bite to eat: her famous Crock-Pot spaghetti. She told me community band practice took place that evening. But, she said, giving me an out, she didn't imagine I'd much want to sit around and watch a bunch of mostly old people play their instruments. Truly, I couldn't think of anything I'd *rather* do. Early on in our friendship, she'd shared with me how she'd taught music her entire working career. Now in her retirement, she sat on the other side of the baton, playing clarinet alongside those she'd taught as kids. The clarinet wasn't her favorite instrument (she played several), but she knew they needed help in that section, so that's what she chose. Over time, she'd e-mailed all kinds of tales about this and that band member, and she always gave me the before-and-after details regarding every practice and performance. I was excited to get to witness one of the cornerstones of her life in action.

Since Dorothy could no longer see well enough to drive at night (nor should she have been driving during the day!), a friend of hers, whom she described as "right nice," drove us to practice that evening. Before we arrived at the school, Dorothy said, "Well now, Charlie Brown, I can't hear well enough anymore to understand which measure the director says to pick it up during rehearsal, so you'll notice the gentleman sitting next to me will point to my music every now and again. I've asked him to give me a hand. He's such a help!"

Yes, I noticed. I also noticed Dorothy's erect posture, her happy smile, and the obvious joy she still got out of being a part of the music. What a grand time we both had!

On the way home from rehearsal—and well before Dorothy's illness was diagnosed—she felt obliged to make another confession. "Welp, Charlie Brown, I don't imagine you noticed this, but I no longer have enough breath left to play all the notes, so I just play the first one in every four. I don't imagine it's much, but it's what I have to give."

Her "one in every four notes" struck a blessed chord in me. *That's what I want to be like when I grow older! Giving what I have to give!* Of course at the time, neither of us had any idea that her notes would ultimately play *so* loudly and profoundly into my heart, into my life—and, years later, spill onto these pages. We did not know that God would soon take her home. We did not have an inkling that her death would come less than two months after the death of my father. Her prayer-filled e-mails were a lifeline for me after he died. Oh, how she encouraged me to *let—*

it—go, "it" being that terrible rage over my father's pain and his seeming inability to deal with it. If only I'd taken her advice, but then . . . I had to learn that deep wisdom in my own time and way. Dorothy's death also came two weeks after my godmother passed. I cannot even begin to explain the utter emptiness of the holes those deaths shot into my life.

While I was still dealing with my father's estate (and all that other muck), an editor who was familiar with my nonfiction books phoned me. She had no idea what I was going through, the three losses I'd just suffered. She left a message on my machine asking me if I had any ideas for senior-citizen characters.

Dad, Johanna, and Dorothy, all gone in a flash. *OH*, how I longed to hear them speak again, to feel the music of their lives swirling around me, lifting me. Where were they when I needed them to laugh with me or collect my tears? Little did Dorothy or I ever suspect that her melodious one-in-four notes, which composed their own beautiful music, had played just long enough within me to inspire not only the fictional Dorothy but an entire series of books to become known as *Welcome to Partonville*.

God's timing is mind-boggling.

❖❀❖

Dorothy played a reed instrument. Dorothy *was* a reed, and the breath of God blew through Dorothy, made music of her, which swirled into my heart.

Thus says the Lord God to these bones,

"Behold, I will cause breath to enter you

that you may come to life."

Ezekiel 37:5 NASB

Charlene was a reed, and the breath of God blew through Charlene, made music of her one-in-four-notes' memories. It went on to play in the lives of thousands. Complete strangers then played their *own* uplifting and encouraging music back into *Charlene's* life in the form of e-mails of praise, notes of appreciation, and tales of the extraordinary ways God touched them through the fictional Dorothy's faith and prayers.

Thank you, my real dearest Dorothy, for being such a remarkable reed. Thank you, God, for putting your lips to her spirit and breathing life into her.

❊ ❈ ❊

Dorothy could have been a bitter and lonesome woman. She could have railed at God about so many things. [MOMENT OF TRUTH: Perhaps she did; none of us knows what truly happens during private moments behind closed doors. But if she did, she didn't get stuck there. She allowed God, in whom she believed, to love her through it, which not only helped her make music, but enabled her to help breathe life back into my grieving bones right after the death of my dad.] She could have given up and turned her back on the music she loved. She could have said things like "I can't see well enough to drive at night, so I can't get to practice. Wouldn't you think all those 'kids' that I taught could oblige me? And I can't hear well enough to know where I'm supposed to pick up the music, so I'm sure not willing to make a fool of myself. Not only that, but I don't have enough breath left to play all the notes, so why bother." But instead, Dorothy *humbled* herself by asking for assistance where she fell short. *I need a ride, please. Can you be my ears, please?* She was such a positive person, who could resist?

Isn't it wonderful to imagine how *your* notes of service, no matter how small, might still be needed? Appreciated? *Transformed* into cantatas? Look what happened here! One never knows what small act of kindness, what small breath of life, you might ultimately help breathe into thousands, when you are willing.

❋ ❋ ❋

Perhaps you feel that what you have to give is no longer—or ever was—enough. Consider what God might create with it, given his way. One small prayer written in a greeting card can change a heart, a course, a life. One small smile or thank-you can let someone know they are seen, valued, appreciated. One small phone call might arrive just when a broken soul most needs the breath of God, and he or she in turn might be encouraged to pass it on.

One small thing. Whatever you have, it is enough, for *all of it is from God*.

Remember, the breath of God does the work, makes the music. We know not where God's breath might blow us or what type of song he intends. But we need to be available, waiting, expectant . . . reed ready.

❊ ❊ ❊

With many reed instruments, the mouth of the musician must be upon it. Such an intimate act, the placement of a mouth near a reed. But then our entire relationship was birthed out of an act of love by the Creator, so why should we shy away from such an intimacy? We are God's offspring, created by love. *Imagine* the passion and intimacy of an act of love powerful enough to create all of humankind. *Imagine* what God might create with you—*through* you (*and the breath of God blew through you . . .*)—as that love continues.

I think back to my time of burnout and my time of unforgiving rage, how I felt like I couldn't breathe. God did not create us to fry ourselves or to hate. Fresh winds cannot blow through that which is not willing. But two years after my father's death, after the letting go of the rage, I awakened one morning at six-thirty from a sound night's sleep feeling the love of God so close to me that the only way I can describe is to compare it to the intimacy of a kiss.

Mouth to reed.

Music.

I picked up my pen and began to write.

Kisses.

Kissing.
Nuzzling fairy touches.
Fluttering breeze lips.
Kissing. Kisses.
Soft, dewy, inch-long breath,
breathing next to the beating
heart in the
crook of my neck.

Kisses.
God, infusing me with all
that matters,
all that is,
all that exists in the entire
all of all,
with a kiss.

Alive. Kissing.
Yes. I remember an

almost kiss hanging,
playfully, temptingly, so close
to my lips. Parted.
Beckoning.
Longing. Holy Spirit,
racing, present and quickened.
white wings, arching, swooping.
Effortless.
Kiss.
I have been kissed.

Cosmic flight. Airborne. Sonic.
Soft.
Very soft Breath
into my nostrils, breathing
breath into me.

Kiss. I have been kissed.
Thus says God
to these dry bones,
I shall cause

breath to

enter you,

and you shall live

by My kiss.

❊❊❊

Yes, sometimes the breath of God arrives in intimate whispers. So, too, can the power of the gift of the breath of life cause us to spiritually *GASP!*—as though God had suddenly dunked us into a freezing river. It is then that his perspective-changing breath flies across our reed-waiting selves and vibrates our entire being.

I offer you this entry out of my memory portfolio as a personal testimony to such a *GASP*. Like my granddaughter sitting on a bale of hay, arms spread, mouth open, I sing this story with truth, abandon, and joy in my heart—for every breath God has given me.

❊❊❊

On rare occasions, George comes along on one of my speaking engagements. Such was the case in 1997 in Flagstaff, Arizona. We decided to tack a few days onto the end of my business trip and just enjoy each other and the scenery. [MOMENT OF TRUTH: We don't always travel well together, but we were gonna try really hard this time.] We'd never been to Flagstaff, but we heard it was beautiful.

With delight, we discovered that the first day of our time alone was also the last day of the Scenic Skyride, located at the Arizona Snowbowl in the San Francisco peaks, and the aspen trees were shimmering with golden beauty. Weather conditions were perfect for a smooth ride and a stunning view, so we purchased our lift tickets, got in line, and began to make our ascent. "Oh, *look* at that!" "Wow! Check *that* out!" It was a glorious ride all the way to the tippy top, where the attendants stopped our seat while we quickly scooted off. The view from the peak was breathtaking.

George decided he wanted to check out a trail off to the left that looked a tad rigorous for me. I was not yet fully rested and recovered from the speaking event [MOMENT OF TRUTH: Read into that what you will] and decided I'd enjoy just sauntering over to the right for a look-see from a different vantage point. We decided we'd meet later at the picnic table near the lift. We parted in different directions and away George went—out of my sight.

After walking toward a prime lookout spot, I realized a slight headache was setting in. Within a few more steps, I began to feel somewhat short of breath. I decided to head toward a small building in front of me. It was closed, but at least I could lean against the porch wall and catch my breath, which, even though I was extremely out of shape, seemed an odd thing to have to do, especially since I'd barely exerted myself. And wow, my head was beginning to *throb*.

I started to lift my left leg onto the step, but . . . I could not lift it high enough. It felt as if my shoe sole were tethered to the ground with a rubber band too strong for my muscles. It ran through my mind that I'd stepped in something, for what else could explain this strange phenomenon? I tried the step up with my right leg, but . . . no go. The exertion seemed to pull the remaining breath from my lungs and I found myself all but gasping in an attempt to fully inhale. I clearly remember thinking, *I need to sit down. I need to sit down. I wish George were here*. I wasn't sure if I could even make it to the picnic table, even though it wasn't more than twenty paces from my location.

I took a couple steps and stopped, took a couple more, lost *more* breath, and for a moment feared I was simply going down. My chest felt incredibly tight. It occurred to me I was having a heart attack. The only way down was the long ride on the chairlift, which likely wouldn't get me to help quickly enough.

It's possible I might die on the top of this mountain! headlined my thoughts.

Odd what transpires when an imminent foreboding of your own mortality crystallizes: a brief calm washed over me. I decided to turn around where I stood to embrace the view—perhaps my last. Tears welled in my eyes as I began to thank God for the magnificent life I'd had and for all the people who loved me—especially him. Between halted prayers of *please look after* and *bless you, God,* the symptom grew worse. And then I simply could not draw a full breath or exhale all the way, not even enough to yell for help. *That* awareness induced a decided sense of panic, the first I'd experienced. *No, Charlene! You cannot panic or you'll hyperventilate, wasting the little oxygen you're managing to intake. You need to calm down.*

In a complete fog, I turned toward the picnic table. I have no idea how I made it to the bench. I remember thinking I might be sick. People were wandering around, but I could not speak. I sat on the bench facing the table (I was afraid I'd keel over if I didn't lie down as best I could), clasped my elbows with my hands, clunked my forearms on the surface, closed my eyes, rested my forehead, which was pounding by now, on my crossed arms, and began to pray a disjointed stream of prayers. *God be with me. Calm me down, Lord. Now I lay me down to sleep . . . Thank you. God be with me. Calm me down, Lord!* I could not for the life of me even shuffle my legs more than a couple inches at a time.

Then I sensed a warm presence along my right side. I felt no movement, just this pressing in, is the best way I can describe it. I detected a faint nuzzle near the side of my breast, as if someone or something were burrowing in. I managed to tilt my head in that direction and open my eyes. The view under my arm was straight into an iridescent pair of calming blue eyes framed by glorious near-white curls. I blinked, thinking I must be hallucinating, but there remained those calming eyes. *I'm dying. But what a beautiful angel God's sent to get me.* I blinked again, this time noticing the entire sweet face of a little girl who was scooted up next to me, leaning into me. Although she wasn't radiating a broad smile, her face was cherubic and her presence was peaceful . . . and intensely calming.

Perhaps I'm already dead.

Then I heard a woman's voice approaching as it called the little girl's name, which I cannot believe I no longer remember, but so it is. I didn't move my head, but I heard and felt and saw the hands of the mother snatching the little girl's comforting presence away from my side. *No, you are not dead . . . yet.* As the mother's voice moved away from me, I heard her reprimand her daughter. I wanted to defend the little girl, beg her mom to let her stay, but no words would come.

Within a moment, incredibly—*miraculously*—the girl was back, sliding across the bench, once again pressing herself against me, burrowing her calmness into me, infusing me with the certainty that God Almighty had his eye on me.

Now came a harsh voice calling the girl. I rolled my head on my arm. The mom profusely apologized to me, saying, "I am *so* sorry! I don't know *what's* gotten into her. I've *never* seen her do anything like this before!" Obviously, Mom worried her child was bothering me. Me, who obviously looked like I was trying to rest. I'm also sure the whole "stranger danger" thing had kicked in.

Away they went, leaving no gap between their departure and George's arrival.

George took one look at me, declared me as white as a sheet, and asked me what was wrong. Whispering, barely audible, I told him I wasn't sure, but that I was glad he was back and that I needed help. I didn't tell him I thought I was near death from a heart attack. I was just so thankful he was there.

"I'll go get help," he said. With my head still on my arm, I could see the tail end of the long line of people waiting to descend, my little blue-eyed angel nowhere in sight.

"I can't stand there," I said, then barely collected enough breath to finish my thought. "I doubt I can even *get* to the lift."

George hustled over to the lift operator, told him I was ill and that we needed assistance. He sent his helper over, who took one look at me, asked me a few questions, then helped George support me upright and get me to the chair, telling those in line he had an emergency. The helper briefly conferred with the lift operator, who told me I was no doubt experiencing altitude sickness and that the antidote was to get lower. There was no other way to accomplish this than by getting me in the chair. He put George in charge of tightly hanging on to me, which he needn't have wasted his breath saying since George had me in a hammerlock.

"When you get to the bottom, don't go to your car. Go straight into the café, ask for water and more water, and don't stop drinking until you get relief from your symptoms. You should start feeling better just by getting lower, but don't forget the water. And keep drinking it. When you feel well enough to travel, go on back down to Flagstaff. But keep drinking water."

Turns out an elevation of 11,500 feet, which we were at when at the top, is too much for me. I should have considered that since even when visiting my son in Albuquerque, which is only 5,000 feet above sea level, I grind through headaches and tiredness for the first couple days, same as I'd done throughout the two-day conference there in Flagstaff, which is at 7,000 feet, one of the highest cities in the United States. Altitude sickness can be fatal.

✳❈✳

When I think back on this incident, which I often do, I cannot help but gasp *spiritually* at the grace and miracle of the calming warm breath God breathed into me through those bright blue eyes in the sweet face of an "I've never seen her do anything like this before" child.

If you could hear the music my reed-vibrating soul makes, if you could feel the rise and swell of the loud symphonic chord of gratefulness I *become* when I embrace the reality of God breathing life into me . . . *OH!* how I feel like an entire gymnasium of a cappella voices sounding the same note of gratitude, especially when I consider that for a moment, when I thought my life was ending, my first instinct was to know—and be grateful for the fact—that I had fully lived, just as God intended.

Ooooooooooooooh!

✳❈✳

We cannot live without breath, which, in the beginning, God breathed into us. We cannot fully live as human beings without our memories (*bless you, memory portfolio!*), wakefulness (*don't miss a single block*), friends (*let them affirm you*), laughing (*at ourselves*), questioning our assumptions (*teachability!*), leaning into life's storms (*balance*), warding off splats (*be good to you*), ridding ourselves of negative thinking (*get sick of listening to you*), trusting our questions (*and God, who has the answers*), awakening our senses (*touch, taste, decorate with rocks*), taking risks (*leap and the net will appear*), firing our imaginations (*ears to hear and time to play*), accepting our successes (*Lands of Odd and Plenty*), letting it rain when it must (*relinquishment*), getting still (*I AM*), and allowing the breath of God to make music of our lives (*living reed ready.*)

Yes, all of the above are obvious; throughout these pages I have undoubtedly told you nothing you don't already know. Likewise, with a little observation and personal story examination, your *own* MOMENTS OF TRUTH, and, most important, the desire to grasp that your one and only life here on this planet *is* better than you think, each of the above qualities is pluck-and-play obtainable. You need neither to be perfect nor to be seeking perfection (in fact, don't!) to live it up; you just need to be real and ready, runnin' what you brung.

I've shared stories about some of the people who influenced my life for the good, and none of *them* was perfect. Mom, Dad, Dorothy . . . they each had their faults and shortcomings. But each of them blessed me *and* God, because they loved, laughed, and lived reed ready. Now it's your turn.

You don't need to approach these life-enhancing targets in order. Just skip right to the reed part, if that tugs at your heart. But I encourage you to make time right here and now (or during your next break) to grab a pencil and take a few thoughtful moments to underline the sections in that long list of a chapter recap that you'd first like to pluck-and-play, or perhaps do so *again*. Reread those chapters. Find the line or two that most grabs you, scribble them down, go sit in a favorite spot and think about them, pray over them, allow them to take root in your soul.

If you don't have a clue where to start, how about rechecking your four sorting lists from the "Let It Rain" chapter. (Gotcha! You should have only *three* left!) Or maybe you should just reread the Humor Hogties in chapter 4, since laughter helps shake lots of things loose. Then again, perhaps you worked the book as you read it and you can already feel the upbeat of God's vibration in your soul, which means it's time to pass the book on to someone else.

But whatever you do at the end of this paragraph, celebrate the fact that you care enough about your life to want not to miss it. I mean it: CELEBRATE! Pour yourself a glass of *whatever* and toast the moment, for in a flash, the next one will arrive and you want to be fully awake and reed ready to capture its glorious possibilities, to tuck its juiciness into your own collection of stories. But before you can capture that moment—one in the string of moments that makes up your life—you've got to LIVE IT! God's breath already stirs within you. When you're ready to work *with* it, LIFE TO THE FULL is yours!

Notes

Chapter 1: Remember When?

1. *Flash Gordon* originally aired as a TV series in the United States in 1954. Black-and-white. Flash Gordon was a "space hero" played by Steve Holland, and the series was based on Alex Raymond's sci-fi comic-strip hero.
2. Annie Oakley for REAL: www.lkwdpl.org/wihohio/oakl-ann.htm; seen by me as a youth on the *Annie Oakley* television series, where Annie was portrayed by Gail Davis.
3. Calamity Jane for REAL: http://en.wikipedia.org/wiki/Calamity_Jane; I first learned of her through Doris Day's portrayal in the 1953 musical movie *Calamity Jane*.

Chapter 2: Wake Up!

1. *Don't Miss Your Kids! (they'll be gone before you know it)* (Downers Grove, Ill.: InterVarsity Press, 1991).
2. Postman Pat and his black-and-white cat, who also came with my prize in a hand-knit version, is a whole wonderful enterprise. www.postmanpat.com.

Chapter 4: Humor Hogties

1. Adapted from a story I first published in *Irish Spirit: Pagan, Christian, Celtic, Global* (Dublin, Ireland: Wolfhound Press, 2002). The book was released only in Ireland.
2. Don S. Skinner, *Passages through Sacred History: Lenten Reflections for Individuals and Groups*, United Church Press, 1997.

Chapter 5: Always Question Your Assumptions

1. First appeared in *Mama Said There'd Be Days like This* (Ann Arbor, Mich.: Servant Publications, 1995).
2. For more information on the Great Dakota Gathering and Homecoming, go to www.diversityfoundation.org/homecoming.html.

Chapter 6: Help! I've Lost My Lean

1. *How to Eat Humble Pie and Not Get Indigestion* (Downers Grove, Ill.: InterVarsity Press, 1993).

Chapter 8: I'm Sick of Listening to Me

1. *The Tao of Willie* (New York: Gotham Press, 2007).
2. Excerpt from *Dearest Dorothy, Help! I've Lost Myself!* (New York: Penguin Books, 2004), 3–6.

Chapter 9: Trust the Question

1. *How to Eat Humble Pie and Not Get Indigestion.*

Chapter 10: Decorating with Rocks and Rockets

1. *The 12 Dazes of Christmas (and One Holy Night)* (Downers Grove, Ill.: InterVarsity Press, 1996).
2. *Daily Ponderables* by Alan Harris, www.alharris.com.

Chapter 11: Leap and the Net Will Appear

1. www.wisconsinducktours.com.
2. www.extremeworld.com.

CHAPTER 14: WHEN IT RAINS, I LET IT

1. A version of this story originally appeared in the January 27, 2007, edition of the *TwinkleGram*, my free e-mail newsletter. Go to www. twinklegram.com to subscribe.

CHAPTER 15: BE STILL AND KNOW

1. Bruce Almighty was a character in the movie *Bruce Almighty*. For a time, God allowed Bruce to have all of *his* power.

2. *Jacob the Baker* by Noah benShea (New York: Ballantine, 1989), 7.

CHAPTER 16: BE A REED

1. Sid Kirchheimer, "Never Get Sick," *AARP The Magaine*, May–June and June 2007.

Acknowledgments

Since this book contains stories culled from a Memory Port-folio containing my entire life, if I thanked everybody who contributed in some way, I'd have to write another book just to name names. Since I'm old now, you can be sure I'd miss at least a couple thousand important people.

So, how *do* I express my heartfelt gratitude? Let me give it a sweeping try.

Thank you, Noah benShea, for allowing God to make music of you. Your inspiring melody of words continues to play in my mind, heart, and purpose.

Thank you, Lorraine Grey Bear, who helped me say and pronounce *Mitakuye Owas.* (Mē-dta-koo-ō-yeh Ō-wa-say) Translation: "All my relatives" or "We are all related." AMEN!

Thank you, Brian Lusk, for going an extra mile to help us "measure the human soul."

If, within the book's stories, you saw your actual name, a reference to your swell unnamed self, or the name to which your name has been changed to protect "the magic," I herewith and gratefully offer you my heartfelt BLESS YOU!

If you did or said anything at any time to awaken one of these stories in my Memory Portfolio, you are appreciated, even if you have no inkling you reminded me.

If, whether before, during, or after, you read this book, you *vicariously* suffer or laugh through any of the *horrid* and *wondrous* dramas I unfolded, kudos for your participation, no matter how unwilling or whole hog.

If you work for Howard Books and have had to deal with me in any way, God bless you specially for your patience and for helping to get this acknowledgment page (and all else, including the cover) into the hands of readers so they can be acknowledged. In other words, thank you, even for helping me to thank YOU!

If you are Cindy Lambert, my editor, let it be known that your gentle guidance made this book exceedingly better. Exceedingly. Thank you for "getting" me and for helping to bring clarity and focus to my heart's passion for this message. Readers, please thank her, too.

If you are my agent, Danielle Egan-Miller, let me publicly HOLLER FROM A ROOFTOP that you are a tenacious, long-suffering, smart, and caring woman, and I ADORE YOU! GOOOOO, Danielle! And Joanna MacKenzie, you rock, too.

If your name is George and you live with me, you are a saint for putting up with me. Anyone who knows us, or anyone who reads this book, already has or will certainly figure that out. But I'm telling you right here and now anyway: I LOVE YOU FOR LOVING ME, even when—*especially* when—I know how difficult I can sometimes make that. Oh, and thanks for letting me share the thermometer story!

If you are one of my sons or grandgirlies, be assured that Grannie B has FULLY LIVED and that you are each a huge-o-rama brightness in that remarkable grace. May your lives be forever and ever full to the brim with freedom, laughter, and grace.

XOXOXOXOXOXOXOXOXOXO

About the Author

If you haven't learned enough about the author by now, you were not paying attention. If you were paying attention and already know WAAAAAY too much about the author, skip the rest of this page and get on with your life!

For those of you who are still with me:

The author is married. If you didn't know this, you haven't read the book yet. Please know I herewith accept and honor your decision to start at the back and work your way forward. After all, it's *your life!*

The author is a mother to two grown sons.

The author is a grandmother to two feisty grandgirlies—which is exactly how she prays they forever-and-ever remain.

The author would love for you to see pictures of many of the things she talks about in this book. Please go directly to the following link, unless you don't want to:

www.dontmissyourlifebook.com.

The author would love to hear from you, she hopes. She can be reached at:

charlene@dontmissyourlife.com.

The author writes fiction, nonfiction, *TwinkleGrams* (*please* subscribe), and notes to herself (the older she gets, the more of those she writes), and tackles any topic that tickles her fancy or imagination.

To subscribe to the *TwinkleGram* and/or learn even *more* about the author, visit:

www.dontmissyourlife.com.